Building School Culture

One Week at a Time

Jeffrey Zoul

Routledge
Taylor & Francis Group
New York London

First published 2010 by Eye On Education

Published 2013 by Routledge
711 Third Avenue, New York, NY 10017, USA
2 Park Square, Milton Park, Abingdon, Oxon OX14 4RN

Routledge is an imprint of the Taylor & Francis Group, an informa business

Library of Congress Cataloging-in-Publication Data

Zoul, Jeffrey.
  Building school culture one week at a time / by Jeffrey Zoul.
      p. cm.
  Includes bibliographical references.
    ISBN 978-1-59667-143-0
  1. School management and organization. 2. Teacher–principal relation-
ships. 3. Communication in education. 4. School improvement programs.
I. Title.
  LB2805.Z684 2010
  371.2—dc22

                                                                    2009043347

  ISBN: 978-1-596-67143-0 (pbk)

Also Available from EYE ON EDUCATION

Improving Your School One Week at a Time:
Building the Foundation for Professional Teaching and Learning
Jeffrey Zoul

The 4 Core Factors for School Success
Todd Whitaker and Jeffrey Zoul

Cornerstones of Strong Schools:
Practices for Purposeful Leadership
Jeffrey Zoul and Laura Link

Leading School Change:
9 Strategies to Bring Everybody On Board
Todd Whitaker

Creating School Cultures That Embrace Learning:
What Successful Leaders Do
Tony Thacker, John S. Bell, and Franklin P. Schargel

Professional Learning Communities:
An Implementation Guide and Toolkit
Kathleen A. Foord and Jean M. Haar

Motivating & Inspiring Teachers, Second Edition
Todd Whitaker, Beth Whitaker, and Dale Lumpa

Help Teachers Engage Students:
Action Tools for Administrators
Annette Brinkman, Gary Forlini, and Ellen Williams

The Principalship from A to Z
Ron Williamson and Barbara R. Blackburn

The Instructional Leader's Guide to
Informal Classroom Observations, Second Edition
Sally J. Zepeda

What Great Principals Do Differently:
Fifteen Things that Matter Most
Todd Whitaker

Professional Development: What Works
Sally J. Zepeda

Dedication

This book is dedicated to Eugene and Audrey Zoul:
děkuji vám za mě naučil tolik o životě.

About the Author

Dr. Jeff Zoul is a School Improvement Consultant with Southern Regional Education Board (SREB) in Atlanta, Georgia. Prior to serving in this capacity, Dr. Zoul served as principal at two award-wining schools, Edgewood Middle School, in Highland Park, Illinois, and Otwell Middle School in Forsyth County, Georgia. In addition to his work as a principal, Dr. Zoul has served as a teacher, coach, and assistant principal at the elementary, middle, and high school levels. Dr. Zoul also served as an adjunct professor of graduate studies at North Georgia College and State University. He is the author of *Improving Your School One Week at a Time: Building the Foundation for Professional Teaching and Learning*, coauthor with Dr. Todd Whitaker of *The 4 CORE School Success Factors*, and coauthor of *Cornerstones of Strong Schools: Practices for Purposeful Leadership* and *Study Guide: What Great Principals Do Differently: 15 Things that Matter Most*. Dr. Zoul has presented at national conferences on a wide variety of educational issues. He earned his doctoral degree from the University of Alabama and holds additional degrees from The University of Massachusetts at Amherst, Troy University, and The University of Southern Mississippi. Jeff is married to Jill, a middle school teacher, and they are the parents of Jordyn. If you would like information about the contents of this book or about inviting Dr. Zoul to speak to your group, please contact him at jeffzoul@comcast.net or (847) 732–1936.

Free Downloads

Many of the tools discussed and displayed in this book are also available on the Routledge website as Adobe Acrobat files. Permission has been granted to purchasers of this book to download these tools and print them.

You can access these downloads by visiting www.routledge.com/9781596671430 and click on the Free Downloads tab.

Contents

Index of CORE Themes

Although the thirty-seven chapters that comprise this book touch on a wide range of educational issues, all of which arise at K–12 schools in the course of the school year, each relates directly to the issue of school culture. School culture is a somewhat intangible concept that includes all aspects of the ways in which educators within a school conduct their daily business. Specifically, a school's culture is impacted by the manner in which those working at the school address the four core factors for school success (Whitaker & Zoul, 2008) of *communication, observation, relationships,* and *expectations.* Each of the Friday Focus memos in the following pages addresses one or more of these four core factors and help to build and promote a positive school culture. These core school success categories are presented below, along with each chapter title that specifically relates to these broad strands. Readers may wish to use this index in addition to the traditional Table of Contents, in searching for information pertaining to a particular theme.

Introduction

In many ways, this book is a followup text to *Improving Your School One Week at a Time: Building the Foundation for Professional Teaching and Learning* (Zoul, 2006), which I wrote shortly after completing my first year as a middle school principal in the State of Georgia. The writings in that book chronicled, to some extent, a year in the life of a middle school, including thirty-seven weekly memos called the *Friday Focus*. Other educational scholars—most notably, Whitaker, Whitaker, and Lumpa (2000)—first used the term *Friday Focus* to describe a staff memo informing teachers and others in the school of upcoming events. The *Friday Focus* memos in this book have a different purpose: they serve as a weekly communication tool, providing insight into a specific aspect of teaching and learning to reflect upon that week and throughout the year.

As principal, each week I wrote—or asked another leader at our school to write—about an issue related to education relevant to all of us who impact student—and teacher—learning. This weekly memo is typically between 800 and 1,200 words in length and was sent out via e-mail to each *teacher* at the school as well as various school officials working in our central office. At our schools, *teachers* included all secretaries, custodians, and cafeteria workers. Because they interact on a regular basis with students, they, too, are teachers and were referred to as such in our schools. I have worked with a number of school secretaries and school custodians who I observed teaching valuable lessons to the students at our school, sometimes simply by the noble way in which they approached their work. During the course of the 2004–2005 school year, we sent out one *Friday Focus* communication each week, compiling thirty-seven such writings in total, all of which are included in my earlier book. Since that time, I continued this practice as principal at two different schools for four additional years, tweaking and refining the *Friday Focus* communication tool with each passing year. In these schools, we found that this practice not only informs teachers of new strategies and best practices, but also builds a sense of collegiality, collaboration, and school pride among staff members. Most importantly, it builds, promotes, and enhances our school's *culture*. Since the publication of *Improving Your School One Week at a Time,* many principals at K–12 schools across the country have written to let me know that they have adopted the *Friday Focus* weekly communication strategy at their schools. Nearly every principal who has contacted me to share their story regarding their experiences with the *Friday Focus* has mentioned that implementing this simple, yet powerful, practice has dramatically—and positively—impacted the culture within the school at which they serve. Such gratifying comments were often accompanied with an equally gratifying question: Are you going to write another version of the book with new *Friday Focus* memos? This book is another glimpse into the life of two schools and their evolving school cultures, as portrayed through a year of *Friday Focus* memos. In rereading these memos, written by me and other teachers and leaders at two different schools—one in Georgia and one in Illinois—it became obvious that the primary benefit derived by writing and sharing these weekly writings was a more positive school culture, thus the title *Building School Culture One Week at a Time*, which stands, in essence, as a companion book to its precursor, *Improving Your School One Week at a Time*.

Again, the title of this book references school culture, in many ways an intangible concept, yet at the same time something that one intuitively senses by merely walking around a school building for any length of time. Hanson (2001) suggests that a school's culture is not visible to the human eye—although its artifacts and symbols, which are visible, reflect the cultural priorities of the school. Definitions of school culture abound and vary widely. Marzano, Waters, and McNulty (2005) found that school culture includes the extent to which there is cohesion among the staff, a sense of well-being among the staff, an understanding of purpose among the staff, and a shared vision of what the school could be like. Senge et al. (2000) calls a school's culture, which encompasses the rules, policies, and procedures of the school, as well as the attitudes, values, and skills that continually reinforce each other, "its most enduring aspect" (p. 325). Senge writes that these attitudes, values, and skills emanate from personal backgrounds, life experiences, and communities to which members belong. Schools are continuously experiencing and undergoing change to the point that change becomes engrained as part of the school culture. Fullan (2001) writes about leading in such a culture of change, suggesting that successful educational leaders "produce the capacity to seek, critically assess, and selectively incorporate new ideas…" (p. 44). School culture can be defined as the product of shared values, beliefs, priorities, expectations, and norms that serve to inform the way in which the organization exists (West-Burnham, 1992) or simply as the "way we do things around here," as Roland Barth has stated on many occasions (2002, p. 6). For the past several years at many K–12 schools in the United States, writing weekly *Friday Focus* memos relating to important teaching and learning issues has become a vital and thriving component of the school culture and has become one of the ways school administrators and teacher leaders "do things." By sending out short memos each week, consistently communicating and reinforcing the best ways to do the many things we are required to do as educators, we are able to slowly—but steadily and methodically—*build* the culture of our schools.

Nearly all the above musings on what constitutes "school culture" refer in some way to the core values shared by those within the school community. Recently, Todd Whitaker and I wrote *The 4 CORE School Success Factors*, a book about our own core values, which, in our experiences, contributed to establishing a positive and productive school culture. These four factors—communication, observation, relationships, and expectations—are vital to the success on any organization and are pillars upon which a school's culture is built. Each *Friday Focus* memo contained in this book, as well as in *Improving Your School One Week at a Time*, relates directly or indirectly to one or more of these four pillars of school success. As we created these 37 weekly communications, we were building the foundation for fostering, maintaining, and enhancing a school culture in which all stakeholders communicated about teaching and learning, observed each other teaching and learning, and established clear expectations for teaching and learning, while forging relationships such that others wanted to meet these expectations. Teachers at these schools became aware of issues impacting them as educators as well as their students. We reflected on what was written in these weekly communications in our faculty meetings and in faculty study groups.

Mary Douglas (1985), an anthropologist, describes a culture as not a static thing, but as a feeling that all within the organization are constantly creating, affirming, and expressing. The *Friday Focus* tool has dramatically impacted the *culture* of many schools that have adopted this practice as a way to consistently and systematically create, affirm, and express the dynamic, emerging, and evolving school culture, with an ultimate goal of school improvement, as measured by increased levels of student—and teacher—learning. Shaping the school culture, providing intellectual stimulation, and communicating effectively are three major challenges facing school leaders. Through the use of weekly teaching and learning memos, such as those contained within this book, we have found a way to effectively and efficiently follow through on many of these important responsibilities that profoundly impact student learning, teacher learning, and school culture.

Although this book is presented in chronological order, beginning with a *Friday Focus* sent out in August and proceeding through a final one in May, I have actually included *Friday Focus* memos from four different school years. Each year, we modified the *Friday Focus* program slightly. For instance, readers will note that several of the weekly memos contained herein relate to a classroom instruction issue beginning with a certain letter of the alphabet. In our fourth year of sending out weekly *Friday Focus* memos, we decided to change the format, moving from weekly memos focusing on random topics to writing about a specific classroom instructional practice. Our inspiration for this idea arose from Barbara Blackburn and her useful book, *Classroom Instruction from A-Z: How to Promote Student Learning* (2007). Each week the author of the *Friday Focus* wrote about a specific instructional issue, beginning with A and moving through the alphabet, oftentimes using Blackburn's book as a resource. Another year, we used 27 of the available Fridays to write about one of Georgia's 27 state standards for school success, explaining the standard, describing how we currently were performing in that area, and suggesting what we could do to become even better. We also changed the way we sent out the *Friday Focus*, at times simply e-mailing the memo, at other times posting it on our school's wiki page and asking all staff to contribute feedback, thereby creating an in-house *Friday Focus* blog. With each passing school year, we changed the format of the *Friday Focus* in a way that best met the needs of our school at the given time. Regardless of these changes, the core purpose of the concept remained the same: to create, maintain, and continuously shape a school culture characterized by staff members sharing their areas of passion and expertise with their colleagues.

For those readers who are unfamiliar with my original book, I invite you to choose anything I have included in this second *Friday Focus* book, modify the content to suit your own school's needs, and send it out to your faculty members. Many of these writings are of a universal theme, applicable to teachers and leaders at any level of education. You may want to begin a similar practice at your school by sending out a few of the writings which follow and then calling on others at your school to begin writing original pieces to share with their colleagues. Readers may choose to skip around, reading those memos that are of greatest interest to them at any given point in time or those that relate to one of the four school success factors of communication, observation, relationships, and expectations. For those readers familiar with my first book's offering of a year of *Friday Focus* memos, I hope this updated version provides you with new ideas for incorporating the weekly teaching and learning communication tool into the way you do things at your school.

As is the case with the first book, this is not a work examining esoteric educational theories or offering scholarly rhetoric. Although all of the ideas presented in this book are based on sound research and years of actual experience, they are simple to understand and relatively easy to implement. This book is designed for use as a resource for educators in improving their schools and positively shaping the existing culture therein. The driving force behind this book is a desire to improve our schools, as Roland Barth (1990) suggests, from within. What follows is a simple, yet step-by-step plan for teachers and principals working together to do just that. We need not necessarily look outside our school walls to find what works; instead, the answer—and the responsibility—lies within each of us who works with students.

1

Laying the Groundwork

The beginning of each new school year is an exciting moment in time for any educator; it is also a day of nearly unparalleled importance. During the first days of a new school year—and even before, as teachers and administrators plan during the summer and throughout any teacher preplanning inservice days—it is imperative that educators set expectations for future learning. Each new school year, students arrive on the first day of school exhibiting their very best behavior. Even those students with the most challenging backgrounds and checkered discipline histories will put forth what, for them, is their very best effort on the first day of school. Parents, too, typically approach the new school year with a positive attitude, anxious to meet their children's teachers and eager to see their children succeed. It is of paramount importance that, as educators, we do whatever we can to capitalize on this once-a-year opportunity while we are still undefeated! We must remind each other of a seemingly trite, yet powerfully prophetic cliché: you never get a second chance to make a great first impression.

Educators must lay the groundwork for all that is to follow during the course of the next 179 school days, making preparations, building the foundation for learning, and anticipating events and obstacles sure to arise and that are better dealt with proactively rather than reactively. Most importantly, the principal and other school leaders must examine the existing school culture and decide as a group in what ways the current school culture is healthy and thriving, working to maintain and strengthen such cultural aspects by reminding all within the school community of these positive cultural norms. In addition, educators within the school must critically examine those aspects of the school culture in need of refinement, improvement, and revisioning in order to achieve a more positive, productive, and learning-focused school environment.

School Culture: Sharing Our Stories

As I mentioned in the introduction, Roland Barth's "casual" definition, oft-repeated, is simply, "the way we do things around here." He does, however, provide a more technical definition of school culture as "...a complex pattern of norms, attitudes, beliefs, values, ceremonies, traditions, and myths that are deeply ingrained in the very core of the organization. It is the historically transmitted pattern of meaning that wields astonishing power in shaping what people think and how they act" (2002, p. 7). The most critical component of this definition of school culture is *shaping what people think and how they act*. The reason that school culture is so vitally important to school improvement is that it gets at the very essence of improving any organization, which is not by changing or improving any specific school program, but by improving the performance of those working within the organization, shaping their thoughts and influencing their actions. High performing school communities accomplish this aim in a variety of ways and through a variety of vehicles relating to school culture. To consider the myriad aspects of school culture, each of which in some way impacts the performance of the people within the school setting, it might help to consider the following framework of school culture, created by Gerry Johnson (1992). Everything included on Johnson's model of culture relates to the "paradigm," which he places in the center and refers to as the set core beliefs which result from multiple conversations and which maintain the unity of the existing culture (Figure 1.1). Every specific aspect of this cultural web surrounding the central paradigm is a topic which can and should be addressed by the principal and other school leaders throughout the school year.

Figure 1.1. Johnson's Culture Paradigm

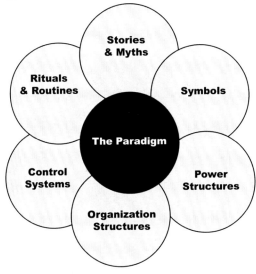

The weekly *Friday Focus* memo is an ideal vehicle for communicating important messages relating to these school culture components. Some of these cultural traits are more tangible than others, but each plays a vital role in shaping the thoughts and actions of each individual working at the school.

The beginning of the school year is a good time to focus on issues more emotional in nature, likely falling under the category of "stories and myths" as opposed to more technical aspects such as "organization structures" or "control systems." In any case, as we lay the groundwork for future success and, perhaps, impending change, it is important that at the outset of the new school year we begin clarifying core values and expectations and start establishing positive relationships such that those working with us will want to meet these expectations.

The First Friday

I believe it is important to share stories that illustrate how the work we are charged with as educators impacts those with whom we work. In sharing such stories, I draw on my own experience and highlight the experiences of specific teachers at the school who have even more moving stories about their personal and professional accomplishments. For the first *Friday Focus* of this school year, I sought to communicate simple, though powerful, stories and quotations that reflect the importance of our work as educators. As is usually the case in the weekly *Friday Focus*, I make reference, in a light-hearted way, to two veteran and excellent teachers. I also share the story of Mike Sloop, an eighth grade science teacher who had been named our school's Teacher of the Year the preceding school year and went on to be selected as Teacher of the Year for the entire school system, comprised of over thirty schools.

In referencing this particular teacher, I write about my belief that his story is one of passion, persistence, and performance—three topics that we had talked about as a school community at length in recent years and topics I knew we would want to revisit and reinforce again throughout the current school year. By this point in time, our school had become celebrated as a school staffed with "passionate" teachers, gaining recognition throughout the district and across the state. "Teaching with passion" had become an oft-repeated phrase at our school, and every teacher knew that my closing to every e-mail I sent out—TWP—stood for "Teach with Passion." In addition, as readers of the first *Friday Focus* book will likely recall, I always tried to incorporate this phrase into the final sentence of the weekly *Friday Focus*, relating it in some way to the week's topic. "Persistence" is another word I wanted to emphasize as we began another year of teaching and learning together. Ours was a high-performing school, yet a significant percentage of our students were faced with a wide range of language, economic, family, and learning challenges. We prided ourselves on doing whatever it took to see that these students succeeded and reminded each other often that persistence was a virtue: We would not give up on our students or each other; regardless of the obstacles we would soon be faced with, urgency compelled us to move forward without accepting failure or excuses. In addition to "passion" and "persistence," I wanted to emphasize the word "performance." At the end of the day, we are all held accountable—increasingly and rightly so—in the world of education today. The teacher of the year whom I highlight below is a popular, enthusiastic, humorous, engaging fellow with an admirable zest for life who is well liked by his colleagues and students alike. More importantly, however, he is highly *respected* by all who know him. Part of this respect is based on the results he achieves each and every year with his students. His performance as a teacher whose students consistently managed to outperform predicted levels of achievement was widely known and hailed throughout our region. Passion. Persistence. Performance. Three *P* words that were already deeply ingrained in the very core of our school culture, yet words we needed to be reminded of as we began another year together. As is typically the case at the beginning of the school year, staff morale was high and we were excited about the days ahead. Yet, before long, typical frustrations would begin to arise and a collective focus on passion, persistence, and performance would help see us through the inevitable obstacles certain to present themselves—sooner, rather than later.

The teachers at our school had worked hard preparing for the first day of school. My goal in this *Friday Focus* was simply to thank them for their efforts, share a brief personal story, share a story about one of our most respected teachers, and remind them of the importance of our lofty, but incredibly difficult, task as educators. I should mention that the personal story I share in the *Friday Focus* below is one I first heard at a church I attended. Some may not be comfortable sharing such personal insights and it may even be inappropriate to do so, depending upon the school and school community in which one serves. At this point in my tenure at this particular school, it seemed an apt and comfortable way to illustrate the point I was trying to make. Of course, there are a multitude of stories each of us has accumulated to share with our colleagues. Educators reading this book must choose those which best fit the current school culture or which are most likely to cultivate the type of school culture they hope to create. What follows is the first *Friday Focus* sent out during a school year, to be followed by thirty-six additional such writings. To establish consistency, we sent the *Friday Focus* out via e-mail (and/or posted on the school wiki) every Friday morning at the same time. Teachers began to anticipate these weekly writings and inevitably responded to them in some way later in the day or the following week.

Friday Focus!

You are not merely here to make a living. You are here to enable the world to live more amply, with greater vision, and with a finer spirit of hope and achievement. You are here to enrich the world. You impoverish yourself if you forget this errand.

— Woodrow Wilson

This week, as we prepared for our kids to arrive on Monday, several of you mentioned that you enjoyed the video presentation displaying motivational quotations relating to our noble profession of teaching and accompanied by musical selections that Bruce created and shared with everyone on Tuesday. Of the forty-eight quotes included, I think the one above most aptly sets the scene for the journey upon which we will all embark next week. No teacher at our school entered this idealistic career path to become wealthy, or because of the plush working conditions, or because of the generous monetary bonuses, or even because they just wanted the chance to hang with cool teachers like Joanie and Jody! Instead, each of us heeded this calling because: (1) we wanted to make a difference and (2) we felt that we had the capability to do so. As President Wilson suggests above, we are here to enrich the world, if not our stock portfolios. We enrich the world each day that we work to fulfill our school mission: *teaching, inspiring, and motivating all learners at our school.*

One way we teach, inspire, and motivate our kids and each other is through storytelling. During the past few years together, many of us have had the opportunity to exchange heartwarming stories of how something we did at our school has had a positive and lasting impact upon one of our students. Often, we were not even aware at the time that we had touched this young man or woman. Like Mike mentioned in his inspiring video presentation at our opening convocation, it is commonplace for our kids to accept our extra efforts without so much as a thank you. Yet years later, that apparent ingrate returns to thank us in what turns out to be a much more meaningful way, which lets us know that we have, indeed, made a difference. Again this year, every teacher at our school will lead with his or her personal vision. For many of us, that is simply doing good work that people will remember. It may not seem as if anyone will remember, but undoubtedly many will.

In introducing Mike to all teachers new to our school system last week, I stated something to the effect that, "Mike will now share just a bit of his own story, which is a story of *passion, persistence,* and *performance.*" Through our *passion* and *persistence,* we directly affect our students' (and each other's) *performance.* I am reminded of a story that a pastor included in the weekly bulletin one week at the church I attended while living on St. Simons Island. It was titled "Pushing Against the Rock." Without going into all the biblical references, it was simply about a man who was commanded to continuously push against a large rock, which he did for many years with no immediately discernible results. After many years of apparent failure, the frustrated man questioned what he was doing wrong and why he had failed. The answer given to him was that he had not failed at all; his calling was to be obedient and faithful and he had exhibited trust in following through on this calling. In the end, he had developed a strong back, arms, and legs through his daily efforts and the rock was moved for him as a reward for his faithful efforts.

Like the man in this story, many of you have mentioned that you consider teaching your "calling," not merely your job. Like the man in the story, many of you will not see the rewards of your daily toil on an immediate or frequent basis. Yet, in the end, you will grow stronger through fulfilling Woodrow Wilson's charge to enrich the world. Just as importantly, so will your students—whether you or they notice it this year or many years hence. Thank you for your passion, persistence, and performance. I am awed to be able to bask in the glow of folks who *Teach with Passion* each day. Have a fabulous first week of school and a…

Happy Weekend!

Jeff

2

A Culture of Care

Schools staffed with teachers who genuinely care about their students—and about each other—are not as common as one would hope and expect. It is very common to find schools in which teachers care deeply about everything that occurs within the four walls of their own classrooms. These are teachers who are passionate about their own subject matter and their own students. A challenge for educational leaders working to create and maintain exemplary schools marked by a collaborative and collegial spirit is to inspire all teachers within the school to expand their vision of care: looking at the entire school community, not only within their classrooms, but beyond, searching for ways to improve student performance in all areas, sharing their expertise with colleagues, and learning from their colleagues at the same time. Schools in which such a "culture of care" is almost palpable immediately upon entering the school facility have cultivated a learning environment in which all stakeholders have an expanded vision of what the school can become.

Schools That CARE

During the year that many of the *Friday Focus* memos in this book were written, our large school system was under the leadership of a new superintendent, Dr. L. C. Evans. In an address to teachers new to the school system, Evans began by sharing his own story, values, beliefs, and goals. A specific point he made during his remarks stood out in my mind, as it aligned so well with the culture we had worked hard to create at our school, a culture marked by a genuine sense of caring for every student and teacher at our school. Evans suggested that successful educators possess this genuine sense of caring to an extraordinary extent and proposed that such educators excelled in four key C.A.R.E. areas: *Commitment, Attitude, Responsibility,* and *Enthusiasm.* Anyone reading this book has likely heard the common saying that people want to know how much you care before they care how much you know. Although this is an oft-repeated phrase in our profession, it still holds true. Caring about the people with whom we work—both our students and our colleagues—is of greater importance in terms of building a positive school culture than caring about curriculum, a specific content area, or any particular program in place at our schools.

Our level of caring evidences itself in many ways, but Evans points out four that seem to capture its essence. Without a doubt, the vast majority of teachers and administrators at every school in our nation are committed to their job, exhibit a positive attitude, feel a sense of responsibility for how well their students perform, and are enthusiastic about what they do and the people with whom they interact. The difference between good schools and great schools is the level of pervasiveness of these four traits. All schools are staffed with educators who exhibit these traits—for the most part. Truly outstanding schools are staffed with educators who exhibit these traits to a nearly-fanatical degree, resulting in *schools that care.*

The Second Friday

Marzano, Waters, and McNulty (2005) found that school leaders who make a difference in student academic achievement fulfill many responsibilities including that of serving as an "optimizer," or one who inspires others by providing an optimistic view of what the school is already doing well and what it can accomplish in the future to become even greater. In the *Friday Focus* memos written early in the year, I try to emphasize this sense of optimism, pointing out specific people within our school who embody what it is we are trying to create as a school. In the following *Friday Focus*, I remark on the good things I had observed while visiting each and every classroom during the first four days of school. I mention four specific teachers at our school who are outstanding, purposely including one teacher new to our school and our head custodian in addition to two teachers who had served as superstar teachers at our school for more than twenty years. In addition to quoting our new superintendent, I also referenced a quote from another of our teachers who had won the systemwide *Teacher of the Year* honor.

Readers familiar with the *Friday Focus* memos know that most begin with a quotation of some sort that relates in some way to that week's theme. For the second *Friday Focus* of the year, I chose to include a quote that makes it incredibly clear just how important our job as educators is. It also gets to the heart of what sets great schools apart from those that are merely good: passionate educators who exhibit caring characteristics not merely for the most part, but with commitment and vigilance on a consistent basis—180 days out of 180 days.

Friday Focus!
_____

Friday, August 22

The future of the world is in my classroom today, a future with the potential for good or bad....Several future presidents are learning from me today; so are the great writers of the next decades, and so are all the so-called ordinary people who will make the decisions in a democracy. I must never forget these same young people could be the thieves and murderers of the future. Only a teacher? Thank God I have a calling to the greatest profession of all! I must be vigilant every day, lest I lose one fragile opportunity to improve tomorrow.

— Ivan Welton Fitzwater

On Monday, I began my twenty-seventh "Opening Day" with a calm confidence that this would be the best one yet. This sense of aplomb derives from the confidence I have in every teacher in our building, from Glenn Chadwick, to Karen Pigott, to Sharon Smith, to Ron Zeliski, and, well, to every adult at Otwell Middle School. As Melissa Sessa shared in her *Teacher of the Year* speech, we all have the opportunity to be a little part of something big because we are teachers. I love this sentiment and the quote above by Fitzwater hints at it, too. Yet, it suggests that our "little" part is "little" only in the sense that it happens slowly, minute by minute, and typically in concert with the efforts of others with whom we work. The "big" opportunities we have to impact the future are the result of thousands of "little" efforts. On Monday, we set the stage for yet another year together leading impressionable young people. I take great comfort in knowing that these impressionable adolescents are at our school, where their minds, emotions, and values are shaped by some of the finest role models in the history of education. These young people will go on to become our future. We will produce many noble citizens who go on to greatness. We also must confront the inevitable fact that others will take a different, even tragic path. All we can do is remind ourselves to *"remain vigilant every day lest we lose one fragile opportunity"* to do whatever we can to encourage the former and reduce the likelihood of the latter. At our school, we will do this both purposefully and intuitively, because our staff has fostered a culture of care which permeates our school. Individually and collectively, the care we have for our profession is palpable.

At Otwell, we are widely known for caring about our curriculum and—even more importantly—caring about our kids. You might enjoy knowing that our new superintendent is similar to his predecessor in at least one way: like her, he cares about kids more than he cares about anything else related to his job. He has made this clear both times I heard him speak. At New Educator Orientation, I heard him remark that he would much rather hire a teacher of average intellect with a superior caring attitude than a highly intelligent teacher with a mediocre attitude. He went so far as to offer an acronym for success as a teacher: *C.A.R.E.—Commitment, Attitude, Responsibility, and Enthusiasm.* Although I concur wholeheartedly with these four keys to success for educators, this is not exactly innovative thinking. Rather, it affirms what we already know at our school: human relations skills are even more important than specific teaching skills or content knowledge. As I visited each classroom in our school this week, I observed each of you setting the tone for a *culture of caring* in your classrooms, classrooms where teachers and students care about learning, care about each other, and care about our community.

The first week of school—indeed, even the first minutes of the first class session—sets the tone for the entire year. If our students leave school today feeling serious and excited about themselves as learners, and about you as their teacher, then, my friends, we are halfway home. From what I observed this week, I anticipate this will be the case. As you progress through the remaining weeks of this school year, I encourage you to reflect on our mission and values. Recall also the import of our charge as quantified by Fitzwater. Remember, too, that our kids will meet any expectations we set for them as long as we are firm, fair, and consistent with these expectations and build relationships with our students so that they will *want* to meet them. Finally, remember that the primary way we accomplish this positive relationship-building with our kids is simply by caring deeply about them as learners and as young people.

Again this year, each of us has a fantastic opportunity awaiting: to be "a little part of something big"…i.e., playing a role in what our own future will look like! Because I work with the best teachers anywhere, I am confident that our kids will make us all extremely proud throughout the year and later in life. Thanks for molding the minds of our future politicians, lawyers, actors, athletes, and religious leaders. May you all be blessed with a healthy and happy year at school and at home. I mentioned on Monday that I honestly think this will be the finest year yet in our school's storied tradition of noted excellence. I offered many reasons, but there are only two that truly matter:

1. Our students

2. The returning and new teachers we have standing ready to teach them, guide them, and care for them.

Understanding the prodigious task of working with middle school students and exhibiting the level of care and commitment necessary to succeed are but two signs that we are committed to *Teaching with Passion* again this year.

Happy Weekend

Jeff

3

Standards for School Performance

Like many school systems across the nation, those in the State of Georgia adopted a new standards-based curriculum in recent years, one in which students and teachers are expected to focus on student performance—what they know and are able to do—at a deep, rather than broad and scattered, level. These new performance standards allow teachers to focus more on teaching to a specific curriculum and less on teaching to a textbook or standardized test. At the same time, statewide assessments were aligned with the new curriculum, taking the guesswork out of teaching and learning for both teachers and students. In Georgia, the new standards-based curriculum—the Georgia Performance Standards (GPS)—was phased in at the K–8 level beginning in 2004 and continuing through 2008, with full implementation being phased in at the high school level through 2012. With the advent of a new and improved state curriculum came a huge effort to train each teacher in the state on how the new curriculum was devised, why it was an improvement over the previous model, and how it would impact instruction and assessment from that point forward. Not surprisingly, this was a daunting undertaking, yet teachers across the state worked hard to learn and adapt to these changes in the very essence of their business: the curriculum.

Although a new state curriculum seemed to consume all available professional learning time for several years, at the same time, the State of Georgia rolled out an equally important set of standards relating to whole-school performance, currently referred to as "School Keys" to success. Whereas the student curriculum described what *students* needed to know, understand, and be able to do, the school standards described what *schools* must know, understand, and be able to do as a foundation for comprehensive, data-driven continuous school improvement (GDOE 2008). Holding teachers accountable for teaching to a prescribed curriculum and holding students accountable for mastering the taught curriculum has gained a great deal of attention in recent years and it can be argued that such a focus on teacher and student accountability has improved both teacher and student performance. It is also important that school leaders work to ensure that the entire school is accountable in a number of areas vital to school success and improvement. Understandably, most teachers are primarily focused on their own curriculum. At the same time, we again must strive to broaden the vision of each teacher at the school, gaining their insights and efforts to improve all aspects of the school, not only those contained within the walls of individual classrooms.

The Third Friday

As I mentioned in the introduction, I served as principal of a middle school that used the *Friday Focus* memo as a way to communicate important messages about all aspects of our profession for four consecutive years. After the first two years of sending out weekly *Friday Focus* memos on random topics each week, we decided to change the format the following two years. For year three of the *Friday Focus*, we devoted more than twenty of the weekly memos to the Georgia School Standards (GSS), those eight broad strands that schools must address in order to not only survive, but thrive, as a learning organization. For the fourth year of the *Friday Focus*, we again adopted a thematic approach, devoting twenty-six of the nearly forty weekly writings to an A thru Z focus on classroom instruction. Many of these writings used Blackburn's *Classroom Instruction from A-Z* (2007) as a resource for sharing specific ideas on how to improve our daily teaching practices. Several *Friday Focus* writings contained in this book are from our fourth year of using the *Friday Focus* as a way to build, maintain, and enhance a collaborative school culture focused on continuous and shared learning. However, I also included a sampling from our third year so I could show how we incorporated the state school standards into our weekly writings as a way to make all teachers within the school more aware of these important school expectations. "Culture" is one of the eight school standards we focused on through *Friday Focus* memos during our third year. The State of Georgia defines school culture as reflecting the "...norms, values, standards, and practices that reinforce the academic, social, emotional, and relational growth of each student and a commitment to the professional growth of all educators" (GDOE 2008, p. 81). Although I have included only three *Friday Focus* writings relating to school standards (an introductory version below, one focusing on curriculum in Chapter 4, and one focusing on leadership in Chapter 16), I sensed that these standards-focused writings informed our staff about our many responsibilities as educators, with each of the writings contributing in a direct or indirect way to fulfilling the standard relating to the State of Georgia's definition of school culture. Principals or other school leaders who have used the *Friday Focus* for more than a year or two may also want to change the format in succeeding years by emphasizing a specific theme each year. Although I have shared only two ideas for doing so in this chapter, the possibilities are endless. Schools could focus on classroom management strategies one year, reading across the curriculum the next, and nonfiction writing the following year. Regardless of the yearly thematic focus, I have found it useful to deviate from the theme periodically throughout the year, perhaps during holidays, testing, parent conferences, or the beginning of a new grading period to write about a topic of timely importance.

Friday Focus!

Friday, August 29

For a particular school to be the launch pad to the levels of success sought by students, it must operate effectively. Whether a school operates effectively or not increases or decreases a student's chance of academic success.

— Marzano, Waters, & McNulty (2005, p. 3).

I hope some of you have had a chance to read the *Friday Focus* book we distributed during preplanning; reading through these again reminded me of the wonderful teachers we have and the many ideas each of our teachers has for improving our school. I even had a parent in the car rider line tell me he enjoyed reading about all the folks at our school who are mentioned throughout the book. That you are willing to share with one another your passion and your expertise is indicative of the collegial and collaborative atmosphere we have in place at our school. Obviously, I have greatly enjoyed the *Friday Focus* writings of the past two years. As we begin our third year together, I thought it would be helpful to continue the practice of writing and sharing ideas through our weekly memo, but with a slight twist. This year, I wanted to dedicate the vast majority of our *Friday Focus* writings to a targeted topic, the Georgia School Standards (GSS). These were previously known as the Georgia Standards for School Performance (GSSP) and are—in a way—a "curriculum for the entire school," that is, what we as a collective group of educators should be planning, implementing, and monitoring throughout this school year and beyond.

The GSS were developed two years ago and are intended to serve as a descriptor of effective school practice for schools in the State of Georgia—or in any state, for that matter. Much of this work derives from *What Works in Schools* by Marzano (2003). The GSS includes eight general strands, or areas for which schools should be held accountable. These eight strands are:

- Curriculum

- Instruction

- Assessment

- Planning and Organization

- Student, Family, Community Support

- Professional Learning

- Leadership

- School Culture

Each of these eight strands is broken down into three or four standards, for a total of twenty-seven standards. This year, through the weekly *Friday Focus*, we will examine one of these standards most weeks. I will ask many of you to tackle one of these standards in a *Friday Focus* writing. Of course, we will have several other Fridays available for any other topics folks might want to write about and share. As for the GSS-themed *Friday Focus* writings, I will kick off next Friday by looking at the first standard relating to the Curriculum strand. Thanks in advance to everyone for becoming familiar with our state's school standards and considering where we currently are in terms of implementing each standard. This should help us in measuring, guiding, and facilitating our work as we strive for continuous improvement.

On another note, thank you all for a wonderful first few weeks of school. Our students and parents have commended you to me throughout this week in the car rider line, at Target, and through many e-mails and phone calls I have received. In addition, one teacher mentioned that our first days of school at Otwell get smoother every year. That is because everyone here is constantly reflecting on past practices and brainstorming ways to continuously improve—both operationally and instructionally. Always striving for greatness is one way that we *Teach with Passion* each day!

Have a well-deserved awesome weekend!

Jeff

4

Curriculum: An Action, Not a Thing

Although many of the *Friday Focus* memos we write during the course of the year relate primarily to cultural issues such as relationship building, establishing shared values, and exploring our attitudes regarding our students, our school, and each other, we never forget that our core business as educators is student academic achievement. As a result, we often write about the three essential and overarching areas which most directly impact such achievement: curriculum, instruction, and assessment. Our curriculum stands as our road map for all that will occur in every classroom in the school each day and must, therefore, be examined regularly to ensure that the taught curriculum is aligned with the intended curriculum. The word *curriculum* has taken on many meanings, including the following offered by Olivia (1997), who suggests that curriculum includes:

- ♦ That which is taught in schools
- ♦ A set of subjects
- ♦ Content
- ♦ A program of studies
- ♦ A set of materials
- ♦ A sequence of courses
- ♦ A set of performance objectives
- ♦ A course of study
- ♦ Everything that goes on within the school, including extra-class activities, guidance, and interpersonal relationships.
- ♦ Everything that is planned by school personnel
- ♦ A series of experiences undergone by learners in a school
- ♦ That which an individual learner experiences as a result of schooling (p. 4).

Obviously, the word *curriculum* encompasses a wide range of items across a spectrum ranging from very narrow to quite wide. However, whether we are examining a single learning objective or an entire program of studies, in order for a school's curriculum to be ultimately effective—that is, students are learning the intended learning standards—we must work to design lesson plans intended to engage students more actively in their own learning.

Learning By Doing

Although a case can be made that learning is inherently active, Chickering and Gamson (1987) suggest that students must do more than listen while in the classroom. They must read, write, discuss, engage in solving problems, and participate in higher-order thinking tasks such as analysis, synthesis, and evaluation. Active learning proponents realize that different people learn in different ways. Educators must purposefully design and plan for daily active learning techniques in which students are discovering, processing, and applying information (Meyers & Jones, 1993).

For many years, Philip Schlechty has been a staunch proponent of focusing more on student work and less on students and teachers themselves. Schlechty (2002) states that there are at least three ways to approach the problem of improving student performance: (a) work on the students, (b) work on the teachers, or (c) work on the work. According to Schlechty, the first two approaches have met with limited success and the key to improving education lies in the third alternative: providing higher-quality work for students that engages them in the learning and enables them to acquire knowledge and learn skills necessary to succeed in our society. As with many aspects of teaching, successfully designing and implementing lessons which authentically and actively engage students in learning curriculum standards requires much more time, effort, and expertise compared to traditional methods, yet the payoff in terms of student academic achievement is worth the investment.

The Fourth Friday

In the previous *Friday Focus*, I merely introduced the eight Georgia School Standards and indicated that we would be examining each of these through the *Friday Focus* memo during the school year. This week's *Friday Focus* looks at the first of the eight strands, curriculum. Each time we introduced a *Friday Focus* writing relating to our school wide standards, we defined the standard, described what full implementation of the standard looked like, and discussed where we were in terms of achieving full implementation and what we needed to do in order to consider ourselves as having reached full implementation of the standard. As always, I began the *Friday Focus* with a quote relating to the weekly theme. For this week's memo, I chose a quote that examines the etymology of the word *curriculum*, suggesting that it denotes action. I used this as a starting point in order to remind teachers to continue our focus on actively engaging students in their own learning. The best way to hold students accountable for learning is not to punish them for failing an exam or failing to turn in an assignment; instead, we hold them accountable by allowing them to take ownership of their learning, discovering more about how they learn and what they need to learn to reach their goals. Although this *Friday Focus* is intended for teachers to reflect upon what the curriculum encompasses and our responsibilities therein, we also strive to motivate students to become more cognizant of and immersed in the curriculum, allowing them to actively run the racecourse that is the curriculum rather than simply having the racecourse shown to them.

Friday Focus!

Friday, September 5

An etymological study of the word curriculum *would likely lead one to the Latin* currere, *an infinitive verb meaning, "To run the racecourse." Curriculum, then, is a verb, an activity, an inward journey, although modern development has reduced the term to a noun, or the racecourse itself.*

— Slattery (1995)

Last Friday, I wrote about the Georgia School Standards (GSS), which, in a way, comprise our entire school's curriculum. The GSS are comprised of eight strands, with "curriculum" standing—not surprisingly—as first on the list and, perhaps, in importance. Once again, the eight strands are:

- Curriculum
- Instruction
- Assessment
- Planning and Organization
- Student, Family, Community Support
- Professional Learning
- Leadership
- School Culture

Curriculum Standard 1 reads as follows: *"The school's curriculum is sequenced and organized to ensure students are taught essential content as outlined in the Quality Core Curriculum or Georgia Performance Standards."* A four-point rating rubric is offered, ranging from "beginning" to "full" implementation with the following description characterizing *Full Implementation*: *"Teachers and administrators have a clear, consistent, and shared understanding of what students are expected to know and understand at all grade levels, as evidenced by student work."*

So, this is the first curriculum standard for our school and what full implementation looks like. Our task, then, is to determine where we currently are and what we need to do to reach the highest performance level possible. I firmly believe that we have made enormous strides in this area in recent years. *"Clarifying what students need to know and understand"* sounds reminiscent of what we are constantly asking ourselves through work in Professional Learning Community teams: What is it we want our students to learn? Next, *"...as evidenced by student work"* is reminiscent of: How will we know if they have learned it? I am convinced that teaching a guaranteed and viable curriculum is the single most worthy means to accomplishing our end goal of raising student achievement. Creating common academic vocabulary lists is one way we can ensure a guaranteed and viable curriculum. Creating carefully crafted common assessments is another. I value so dearly the many individual talents we have among our esteemed faculty roster. Yet, I also recognize that we all must agree on what must be taught and—alas!—what must be eliminated from our endless supply of things we would *like* to teach. Those standards included in the state curriculum simply must be taught. More importantly, of course, these standards must be *learned*, which brings me, in closing, to the quote above.

Thank you for engaging our students in our core work: teaching and learning the curriculum. Each of us has ruminated more than once on how to hold kids accountable for their learning. We shoulder this responsibility for them at the outset by committing ourselves to teaching a guaranteed and viable curriculum. Next, we must get them to *run the racecourse* that is our curriculum; merely handing the racecourse to them and covering every turn and straightaway is not enough. Initially, at least, viewing *curriculum* as a verb, rather than a noun, makes our already daunting task even more taxing as we design new ways to ensure engagement, choice, variety, and learning. Soon, though, we notice the difference and our jobs actually become easier—and more fulfilling—as we observe our kids running the racecourse (i.e., become engaged in and accountable for their learning) for themselves.

Like most rewarding things in life—and nearly everything associated with the noble profession of education—motivating students to *run* the course rather than *covering* the course for them requires hard work. Yet, the resulting fun makes the journey worth it—both for students and teachers—and is one way that we *Teach with Passion* at our school!

Have a stupendous weekend!

Jeff

5

Active Learning

The Fifth Friday

In the previous chapter, I mentioned that we have tweaked the format of the *Friday Focus* from year-to-year, incorporating a theme to connect the majority of the weekly memos throughout the year. Although we focused on our state's school standards one year, we moved to a focus on classroom instruction from A–Z the next. Beginning with this chapter, I have included several of these instructional A–Z *Friday Focus* memos within this book. Some are ones I wrote myself, whereas others are ones that were written and sent out by teachers or other administrators.

For the first installment of the A–Z instructional theme, I wrote about a topic directly related to what I touched on in Chapter 4: active learning. The quote by Bruner that introduces this week's *Friday Focus* says it all: Students who are actively engaged in learning material not only recall that information more readily afterwards, but are also more likely to be able to apply the learning they have acquired in different contexts. Near the end of this week's *Friday Focus*, I make reference to the daily announcements at our school. I began the daily announcements each day immediately after the first morning bell sounds and tried to limit these to no more than three to five minutes. However, I did incorporate one phrase to end the announcements each day, reminding students that regardless of anything else that is occurring, they should "work hard, have fun, and be nice" today. In my experience, the first two of these three daily reminders apply to active learning. In classrooms where students are engaged in active learning behaviors, not only are they likely to learn more, they are also likely to have more fun. Anytime we can make learning fun, we increase the chances that students will strive to learn more. In addition, when students are engaged in fun and active learning, they are actually working harder than they would if they were passively taking in information delivered by the teacher. Somewhat ironically, the harder they work, the more fun they have—and the more they learn as a result. Too often in our classrooms, teachers are the ones doing all the work. We must shift this workload to our students by emphasizing active learning strategies whenever possible.

Friday, September 12

A is for active learning

Students who actively engage with the material are more likely to recall information later and be able to use that information in different contexts.

— J. S. Bruner (1961)

This year marks our fourth year of writing and sharing our thoughts about teaching and learning through the *Friday Focus* format. Each year, we have tweaked this professional writing and sharing opportunity just a bit. As you will recall, last year we devoted many of the *Friday Focus* memos to examining the Georgia School Standards. This year, our focus will return to classroom instruction, as we work through the alphabet, writing about some aspect of instruction related to each letter of the alphabet, from A to Z. For many of these, we are using Barbara Blackburn's book, *Classroom Instruction from A–Z: How to Promote Student Learning* (2007) as a reference.

In kicking off the A–Z schedule, I relied on Blackburn's text for an idea related to the letter A: **Active Learning**. As Bruner suggests above, students who are actively involved in their own learning are more likely to both recall and use such learning later in life. What constitutes "active" learning? Certainly, much of what we have learned over the years at the system level through our *working-on-the-work* (Schlechty, 2002) focus relates to the concept of active learning. It encompasses a host of characteristics, but is most pointedly evidenced when students are authentically engaged in the lesson. Blackburn (2007) suggests that such engaged students exhibit several key characteristics:

A Attention

C Concentrated Effort

T Thinking

I Involvement

V Variety

E Engagement

All of the above are obvious components to and requirements for engaged learning. Interestingly, they are also necessary components to *engaged teaching*. Active learning requires that both the student and the teacher become involved in the learning activity. As a classroom teacher myself for twenty years, I still reflect back on my own strengths and weaknesses in the classroom. I honestly think that I was a master at being actively involved in each and every lesson as the teacher. Alas, I was deficient in ensuring that my students were equally active. On the other hand, we have all known teachers whose students were very "active" but not necessarily in a way that was related to learning, rather than random, outcomes.

Each day on the announcements, I talk about working hard and having fun. In my own life, these two actions have always gone hand in hand. If we make learning fun, we are sure to produce excellent student work and active learners. If we can make the learning meaningful and relevant, we are much more likely to actively engage our kids in learning. Finally, if we establish routines and expectations, we can encourage our kids to take an active role in their own learning. Our kids must take an active role in their own education; it is up to us to cultivate this accountability within them. Gain their **A**ttention at the outset of every lesson; require a **C**oncentrated effort on their part as well as your own; inspire them to **T**hink critically; plan carefully to ensure their **I**nvolvement; and offer a **V**ariety of learning tasks during each class session. By doing so, we will achieve active and authentic **E**ngagement in our classrooms. These gifts will stay with our kids ages and ages hence.

Understanding what active learning looks like and what it requires of us, as educators, is another way we commit to *Teaching with Passion!* again this year.

Happy Weekend

Jeff

6

Background Knowledge: The Foundation

For Future Learning

The terms *background knowledge* and *prior knowledge* tend to be used interchangeably and have become increasingly familiar in recent years to educators striving to meet the needs of students by building from their current areas of strength in order to advance their learning to new heights. These terms can be defined in many ways, including the following by Biemans and Simons (1996): "...all knowledge learners have when entering a learning environment is potentially relevant for acquiring new knowledge" (p. 6). Students who lack sufficient background knowledge or who are unable to activate this knowledge will likely struggle to access and progress through the curriculum. Prior knowledge has a significant influence on student performance, explaining up to 81% of the variance in posttest scores (Dochy, Segers, & Buehl, 1999). By implementing specific strategies to support students' background knowledge, educators can better support students' content area learning.

Building a Common Academic Vocabulary

Students vary widely in the levels of vocabulary with which they are familiar upon entering any new grade level or academic course. This is one specific example in which their previous knowledge about a subject will likely impact their future learning about that same subject. Students who lack understanding of and fluency in basic academic vocabulary in a content area will have a difficult time constructing new understanding and adapting existing conceptions and beliefs as necessary. Marzano and Pickering (2005) developed a comprehensive and systematic program for building academic vocabulary across grade levels. After studying this model, several teachers at our school decided to implement a similar program for creating common academic vocabulary lists in all content areas in grades 6 to 8 at the middle school where I served as principal.

In departmental meetings, teachers worked together to create lists of thirty words for each grade level in each academic content area which teachers would teach and students would master by the end of the school year. Our commitment was that a student who attended our school for all three grade levels would master ninety academic content words in the areas of math, social studies, science, and language arts. The process began with a great deal of productive debate, as department members determined at which grade level each word should be "owned" as many of these words are ones that arise at all grade levels. Ultimately, each department agreed upon three separate lists of words to be mastered, one each for grades 6, 7, and 8. We called these lists of academic vocabulary our "30 on the Wall." We created poster-size 30-on-the-Wall word lists and placed these posters in the same location in every classroom in the school so that visitors would see, for example, the "30 on the Wall" for a sixth grade science class in the same corresponding location as the "30 on the Wall" for eighth grade social studies upon visiting that classroom. Teachers then referred to these lists throughout the school year, reminding students each time they discussed one of the thirty content words. In addition to creating common word lists for each content area, we also decided to create what we called a "Universal 30," which became a list of thirty learning verbs we expected students to engage in while learning in any classroom at our school. Words such as *compare, solve, analyze,* and *create* were included as learning behaviors we expected to observe in all classrooms throughout our school.

Creating common academic vocabulary lists and ensuring that all students in the school master such lists is but one way to make certain that all students gain specific knowledge about the content we must teach and they must learn. Direct instruction designed to build on background knowledge so as to increase future learning is one way we can support all learners at our school, regardless of where they are when they arrive.

The Sixth Friday

As we moved to the letter B in our A–Z journey through classroom instruction, for this week's *Friday Focus,* I relied on Blackburn (2007) as a reference for reminding teachers of the importance of building on the prior knowledge our students possess—or do not possess—upon entering our classrooms at the start of each school year. I shared several specific ideas Blackburn has used successfully to activate students' prior knowledge. I also used this opportunity to remind our teachers of the work we had done as we studied this concept the previous school year, ultimately creating our 30-on-the-Wall lists of academic content vocabulary. In addition, readers will note in this week's *Friday Focus* that when I originally sent out this memo, I also attached three handouts relating to building academic vocabulary. This is something that we did periodically in our *Friday Focus* writings. Generally, I avoid attaching handouts, as I want the *Friday Focus* to be short enough for every teacher to read in a single setting and to be something that they will read immediately, without putting it off to the side. Still, at times, I—or another *Friday Focus* author—might refer our colleagues to a handout that can be used in their classrooms, a website they can use for additional resources, or our school's computer share drive to which they can refer to access further documents relating to the week's theme. Although I guard against detracting from the succinct overall message of the *Friday Focus*, it can be helpful to direct interested teachers to additional resources they might use to learn more about the week's topic.

Friday Focus!

Friday, September 19

B is for Background Knowledge

Although the extent to which students learn new information is dependent on many factors, research supports one compelling fact: What students already know *about the content is one of the strongest indicators of how well they will learn new information relevant to the content.*

— R. J. Marzano (2004)

Last Friday, I wrote about Active Learning as an instructional focus for the letter A. In Barbara Blackburn's book, *Classroom Instruction from A–Z: How to Promote Student Learning* (2007), the author chooses "Background Knowledge" as the chapter topic for "Chapter B." I was excited that this was her topic for the letter B partly because of my passion for Marzano's work related to building background knowledge and, especially, building academic vocabulary (BAV). For those who are new to our school or may have forgotten this method for teaching academic vocabulary, I am attaching the BAV handout we created last year, along with the six steps for introducing new academic vocabulary (Marzano & Pickering, 2005), a student progress chart, and a description of vocabulary knowledge level ranging from 1 to 4.

Blackburn calls background knowledge—or the knowledge our students already have—the foundation for any new learning they will acquire. We need to know what our kids already know (or think they know) before we can build on that foundation of learning, taking them from where they are, to where they need to be. She offers a few strategies for understanding and building this background knowledge. The most common way is a KWL or a variation she calls LINK:

L *List* everything you know

I *Inquire* about what you want to know

N *Now* we are going to take notes

K What do you *Know* now? (p. 9).

In addition to these familiar methods of building upon background knowledge, Blackburn shares two other simple ideas worth mentioning: (a) *Sticky Notes:* As students enter class, hand them a sticky note. A question on the board asks them to write what they know about a new topic to be studied. Students respond on sticky notes and place on the board. The teacher reads every sticky note, verbally acknowledging each, perhaps categorizing them on the board, before moving forward with additional teaching and learning about the topic at hand; (b) *Sharing What We Know:* Have students work in small groups to write facts about a particular topic on a sheet of paper. As the paper comes around, each student writes one thing they already know about the topic and passes it along to their neighbor. The paper continues around the small group circle, a second or third time, if appropriate. When the group has exhausted all thoughts, have groups switch papers, reading another group's list to see whether they can add to it. They will more than likely see something new, too, that they had not thought of.

Background knowledge is the foundation for all future learning. Our students come to us with wildly varying levels of background knowledge based on the number and frequency of academically-oriented experiences they have had and their ability to process and store information. Outside of school, we are not able to influence the former, but we have a huge impact on the latter. We must discern where our students are before we can advance them to a new level of understanding. Students will retain information better if we connect it to those prior experiences they might have. There are many strategies we can employ to learn where our kids are and how we can best connect where they are to where they need to be; thanks for incorporating these into your instructional practices.

Understanding what our students already know and connecting this background knowledge to new information we want to present is another way we commit to *Teaching with Passion!*

Happy Weekend

Jeff

7

Differentiated Instruction Defined

A primary challenge facing teachers at many schools today is finding a way to effectively and efficiently meet the widely varying needs of all students within their classrooms. More than ever, students enroll in courses with vastly different levels of both innate and learned abilities pertaining to the curriculum of a particular course. Teaching a class of twenty-five or more students may well require teaching students with twenty-five distinctly different levels of reading, writing, and critical-thinking capabilities. Even in high schools where students are more likely to be grouped by ability level, teachers face tremendous challenges meeting the various linguistic, cultural, and social differences that are likely to exist among their students. To cope with these differences in learning styles, abilities, interests, motivation, experience, and rates, teachers must learn to differentiate instruction in a way that is helpful to all learners—and manageable for the classroom teacher. Teachers who *make* a difference *plan* for differences among the students they teach.

Making a Difference

Students in our nation's schools across all grade levels differ in an infinite number of ways. To categorize these differences broadly, Tomlinson and McTighe (2006) classify student differences as falling into three areas: differences in readiness, interest, and learning profile. Differences in *student readiness* include a student's proficiency with specific knowledge, understandings, and skills. Such differences affect a student's growth as a learner. Differences in *student interest* relate to the differences we see within our students corresponding to their current inclination toward and engagement in a specific area of study. The level of interest a student has in a topic impacts their level of motivation to learn more about the topic. Finally, differences in one's *learning profile* include a student's preferred mode of learning and processing. Student learning profiles are influenced by gender and culture as well as learning style and intelligence preferences.

Our best teachers have broken through the one-size-fits-all mentality of curriculum design and delivery of instruction. Whether at the elementary, middle, or high school level, such educators realize that our primary charge is to teach students, not content. Teaching students first and programs second includes planning for the differences we are sure to see within these students and acting in strategic ways designed to accommodate such differences. In virtually every school, we can find at least one teacher who excels in differentiating instruction this way. In our very best schools, educators have worked to make sure that differentiated instruction is not merely practiced sporadically or haphazardly, but have broadened its scope to the point that it is a fully ingrained component of the school's culture: All teachers are committed to planning for—and embracing—differences among the students they teach and responding in a way that maximizes student learning, making a positive difference in the achievement of all students, not just those who fit our preconceived notion of where students should be when they arrive in our classrooms.

The Seventh Friday

As I mentioned before, the *Friday Focus* memos in this book are ones that were written at two different middle schools where I served as principal. Although these two middle schools were very different in many ways, they also shared many challenges. One such challenge was teaching teachers how to effectively differentiate instruction for their students. Although some teachers at both schools seemed to accomplish this intuitively, the majority struggled with the concept as well as the practice. The struggles we experienced related less to their willingness and more to the actual practice: Teachers at both schools wanted to know what differentiated instruction really meant and how they could best implement differentiation strategies. Because this was going to be an ongoing point of emphasis at our school, I decided to start with the basics in this writing and follow up in future *Friday Focus* writings, as well as with further training in staff meetings and on professional learning days. For this first writing, I focused on what differentiated instruction (DI) is—as simply and precisely as I could. I define the practice, explain the four ways we can differentiate instruction, and share the benefits our students realize by our using DI. Finally, I mention something not uncommon in my *Friday Focus* writings: I am in no way an expert on the topic under discussion and I will need to rely on our teacher leaders who have greater expertise than I to help ensure that DI becomes part of our school culture rather than something practiced in isolated classrooms throughout our school.

Friday, September 26

$\mathcal{D}$ is for Differentiation

What we share in common makes us human. How we differ makes us individuals. In a classroom with little or no differentiated instruction, only student similarities take center stage. In a differentiated classroom, commonalities are acknowledged and built upon, and student differences become important elements in teaching and learning as well.…Students have multiple options for taking in information, making sense of ideas, and expressing what they learn. A differentiated classroom provides different avenues to acquiring content, to making sense of ideas, and to developing products.

— Carol Ann Tomlinson (1995)

I readily confess to knowing much less about differentiated instruction (DI) than many other educators. Much of the learning I have acquired regarding DI, however, was acquired as I gained my Gifted Certification along with twenty-eight teachers on our staff several years ago. One profound takeaway from that experience—which was an eye opener to many of us—was the realization that teaching gifted students and teaching students with learning disabilities is more alike than different and *very similar* in that effective teachers in either role are extremely adept at differentiating instruction so as to accommodate varying levels of abilities within the classroom. Defined in its simplest form, DI is an approach to teaching that is based on a philosophy that *expects* student differences in learning and *believes that teaching should be adjusted to these differences*. The intent of DI is to maximize each student's growth and individual success by meeting students where they are and assisting them in moving forward.

Another idea we learned about DI through our gifted coursework, which I am sure is merely a reminder for returning Edgewood teachers, is that there are four ways to differentiate instruction. We can: (a) differentiate the *content*; (b) differentiate the *process*; (c) differentiate the *product*; and (d) differentiate the *learning environment*. Looking ahead, Joanne, Erin, and I learned at our meeting last week that we will be engaged in content area differentiation learning/work during the afternoon session of our November Institute Day. I am sure we will review our basic understandings, such as the four ways to differentiate, before getting down to the deeper work of differentiating units of instruction and using preassessments to enable differentiation to occur.

Prior to our work in November, though, I do want to get the ball rolling at our school in terms of discussing, however briefly, the importance of DI in education today. Years ago, many of us "solved" the "problem" of student differences by "teaching to the middle." We quickly learned the inefficacy of such an approach. This style of teaching left struggling students behind while failing to engage advanced students. Today, most of us realize the need to differentiate in order to ensure learning for students of all abilities. Yet, accomplishing our work in this area is not easy, even for the most willing teacher. DI is difficult, requiring us to plan carefully and assess constantly. My hope is that together we can work to achieve our goal of successfully differentiating instruction for students in all classrooms at every grade level. I have asked Erin Tracy-Lambrecht to write a future *Friday Focus* on the topic of DI. Erin knows far more than I about this critical area of student learning and she has graciously agreed to share her wisdom through the FF. Thanks to her and to all our resident experts who I hope will share what they know throughout this year and beyond.

Although DI can be challenging, practiced consistently and effectively, it results in benefits, both to *students*...

1. Every student has an opportunity to succeed which is enough for them to approach new learning situations with confidence and motivation;

2. Every student has an opportunity to discover personal strengths and show multiple intelligences; and,

3. Students experience less frustration relating to confusion or boredom.

...and *teachers*:

1. A greater understanding of each student's learning progress;

2. A greater sense of control over each student's learning progress; and,

3. The reward of having a classroom that allows equal opportunity for success for all students.

The late Dr. Carole Morreale, formerly with Lake Forest schools and Northwestern University, was highly regarded as an expert on gifted education. As such, she spoke, wrote, and taught about DI. I enjoy the following quote attributed to her:

> If I'm [the teacher] doing a good job, you [the student] will be struggling appropriately. Define what is fair for each student. Fair is when

each student is struggling just enough to learn something new. A fair fit for one student will be different from the fair fit for another. A simple packaging for differentiation is this: put students in situations where they don't know the answer—but are able and willing to find it (Wilmette District 39, 2008, p. 1).

Recognizing variance in student background knowledge, readiness, language, preferences in learning, and interests—and reacting responsively—is another way that we *Teach with Passion!* at our school.

Happy Weekend

Jeff

8

Expecting the Best

Each school year, the first days and weeks are critical in setting the tone for all that will follow. Perhaps the most important message educators must communicate at this vitally important time of year is their expectations. Principals must make clear to every staff member at the school their expectations in a number of areas. Teachers must establish and communicate firm, fair, and clear expectations for every student in their class. Teachers and administrators must also work together to create schoolwide expectations for student behavior and learning, as well as expectations they have for each other. After establishing these various expectations, teachers and administrators must diligently adhere to them on a consistent basis, monitoring teacher and student performance to ensure that all within the school are acting according to agreed upon standards. Existing research on the importance of setting and adhering to preestablished expectations is vast, and includes research by Edmonds (1986), who found that schools that establish high expectations for all students and provide support necessary to achieve those expectations have high rates of success in several measurable areas.

Getting What We Expect

For many years, I have repeated a saying I heard years ago when coaching basketball: "Whether you think you can or think you can't, you're right." In other words, our expectations determine our level of success. Obviously, our expectations must be attainable. Although I run regularly and have completed several marathons, I cannot expect to win the Boston Marathon. I can, however, set expectations for myself that I will run several miles every other day and complete any race I enter, and improve my time from race to race. Similarly, not every student can be valedictorian and not every student will have a spotless discipline record, but expecting students to behave according to a clearly defined student code of conduct, expecting all students to learn grade-level-appropriate material, and expecting all teachers at the school to uphold these expectations is not only possible, but necessary, to achieve optimal results.

Teacher expectations can be self-fulfilling. The power of belief one person has in another can become a propelling force for that person to begin believing in himself. Although intellectual ability obviously affects student academic performance, hard work and effort are even more important in determining a student's level of performance. Most educators would agree that their own success was a result of hard work and effort. As educators, we must continue to communicate this message to students, expecting them to achieve at high levels as a result of their work and effort, rather than any innate ability. We must offer more than platitudes in this area, using this *belief* that all students can and will succeed as a launching pad for *actions* designed to ensure that they do. If educators are truly committed to creating schools in which all students learn at optimal levels, they must not only *expect* the best, but also *inspect* what they expect on an ongoing basis to ensure that every adult in the school communicates and adheres to crucial messages, such as: (a) The work we do is important; (b) You can do it; and (c) We will not give up on you (Howard, 1990; Saphier, 2005). Over time, students will recognize that every teacher in the school stands together on these core messages and we will begin to get what we expect: their very best performance.

The Eighth Friday

By this point of the school year, of course, we had already discussed and agreed upon expectations for our students and each other. However, the school year was just far enough along to remind teachers of the importance of these expectations. Some students who at the beginning of the year were behaving perfectly and turning in all assigned work were starting to slip just a bit. Likewise, some teachers were getting out of the habit of maintaining an active presence in the hallways during transitions or not following through on consequences for subpar student performance. The letter E in our A to Z focus on classroom instruction arrived at a propitious time, then, although, truthfully, any time in the school year is an appropriate time to remind others about the importance of expectations.

In an earlier work, Todd Whitaker and I (2008) listed and described four guidelines that effective schools follow in terms of expectations. Educators at such schools must (a) establish and communicate clear expectations for all, (b) consistently clarify, reiterate, and reinforce these expectations, (c) serve as a role model by acting in accordance with established expectations, and (d) monitor their commitment to established expectations. As with anything worthwhile that we do in education, achieving optimal levels of learning for all students and consistently superior teaching performance on the part of all teachers is not easy and setting high expectations is merely a starting point. Schools that make an impact in this area go beyond setting high expectations; they follow through on these expectations, monitoring them regularly and turning them into commitments by insisting that all educators throughout the school adhere to and model school expectations for success.

In the following *Friday Focus*, I follow a familiar format. After starting with a relevant quotation, I mention two teachers at our school in a positive light, tying in their laudable attributes to the week's topic—if every one of our students had parents like these two, our expectations for student success would be sky high. Next, I spend the bulk of the writing focusing on the topic itself, sharing personal ideas and research related to expectations. Finally, I close by again highlighting a few more teachers at our school who excel in the area of establishing and maintaining clear and appropriate classroom expectations. I also suggest that other teachers stop by these rooms to observe these teachers in action, completing one of their monthly peer observations at the same time.

Friday Focus!

Friday, October 3

E is for Expectations

A teacher's beliefs about students' chances of success in school influence the teacher's actions with students, which in turn influence students' achievement. If the teacher believes students can succeed, she tends to behave in ways that help them succeed. If the teacher believes that students cannot succeed, she unwittingly tends to behave in ways that subvert student success or at least do not facilitate student success. This is perhaps one of the most powerful hidden dynamics of teaching because it is typically an unconscious activity.

— R. J. Marzano (2007, p. 162)

Imagine if every one of our 912 students had, say, Phil Westray for their father and, perhaps, Beth Richardson for their mother. How would you expect these students to perform and behave? I think we would all expect a school full of respectful, hard-working, high-achieving future valedictorians involved in numerous extracurricular activities. Would that all our students were so blessed as to have parents like Beth and Phil, making it obvious to us what we should expect from them—nothing less than the absolute best! Perhaps our true calling in education is to hold ourselves and all our students accountable for such superior performance. Expectations are a critical component of what we do. Truthfully, unbelievably great students like Cole and Cody and Katie stand out as exceptional young people in every way. Although we have all helped them grow, they succeed primarily as a result of loving parents who hold their own lofty expectations for their children. Although not every student will realize that level of success, we can and should expect each of our students to succeed at the very highest level possible for them as individuals—even knowing that, in many instances, we are the best adult role models and parents they may have in their lives.

Anyone who has spent any amount of time talking with me about education knows that my core charge to educators is simply this: we must clearly establish high expectations for students and then set about building relationships with them such that they will want to meet our expectations. Although this is mere hunch based on twenty-six years of teaching experience, as opposed to any exhaustive research I have conducted on the topic, I suspect that nothing influences how well our students perform in terms of academics and behavior as much as the expectations we hold for them and the firm, fair, and consistent manner in which we adhere to them. Probably the most famous study in the area of teacher expectations for students is Rosenthal and Jacobson's *Pygmalion in the Classroom* (1968) in which teachers were told at the outset that 20% of their students (randomly selected) were identified as "spurters" whose academic performance would likely grow dramatically during the year. Sure enough, at the end of the year, these 20% significantly out gained the 80% who were not identified as "spurters" on an academic achievement test.

Marzano (2007) discusses two categories of teacher behaviors that communicate expectations to students: *affective tone* and *quality of interactions* with students. Affective tone refers to the extent to which teachers establish positive emotions in classrooms. In terms of quality of interactions, research shows that teachers differ in their interactions with high- versus low-expectancy students. To avoid differential treatment in terms of affective tone, Marzano suggests examining whether we treat "low-expectancy" students differently by:

- Making less eye contact
- Smiling less
- Making less physical contact or maintaining less proximity
- Engaging in less playful or light dialogue

Relative to quality of interactions, he suggests examining whether we treat low-expectancy students differently by:

- Calling on them less
- Asking them less-challenging questions
- Not delving into their answers as deeply
- Rewarding them for less-rigorous responses

In reflecting on my own teaching career, I fear that I may have been guilty of several of the above differences in treatment of students for whom I held lower expectations. My intentions were not malicious; rather, I thought I was doing "lower" students a favor by letting them off the hook at times. Of course, as Marzano suggests, this thinking—although well-intentioned, perhaps—was folly. We must work to communicate high expectations for *all* students.

Blackburn (2007) also addresses expectations and suggests there are three ways to incorporate high expectations in your classroom: (a) through your words; (b) through your actions; and (c) through your expectations of one another in the classroom. The language we use with students clearly reflects our beliefs. Students will follow our model when they hear us using excuses or saying we can't do something. Even more important, our actions must show that we expect all students to learn. By calling on all students and making all students demonstrate their understanding of the content, we are communicating our expectations through our actions. Finally, we must cultivate a classroom culture whereby students expect each other to learn, participate, and behave properly. Through our modeling, students can learn to reinforce positive learning and behavioral actions for each other.

Many students at our school have absolutely no vision of anything other than where they are right now. We can help our kids create a different vision for themselves through our words (including affective tone) and actions (including quality of interactions). Many teachers at our school are obvious masters at expecting their students to perform in a certain way and holding them accountable for doing so. I have already highlighted Tony Jones several times in this area. Rachael Auyer also comes to mind immediately, as do Catherine Keyser and Ronnie McNeese. Like all of us, Tony, Rachael, Ronnie, and Catherine begin the year by establishing clear and specific routines and outlining what and how students will learn as the year progresses. In a matter of days, their students are well on their way to learning more than they ever thought possible. If you have a chance, stop by their classrooms for a peer observation visit soon or invite others to see how you use expectations to influence outcomes in your own classroom. Understanding that our expectations for students influence outcomes and acting accordingly is another way we commit to *Teaching with Passion!* at our school each day.

Happy Weekend

Jeff

9

Graphic Organizers

The term *graphic organizer* can be defined as "...a visual and graphic display that depicts the relationships between facts, terms, and/or ideas within a learning task..." (Hall & Strangman, 2002, p. 1). Using graphic organizers has gained momentum among educators as a specific way to improve instruction, making our curriculum more accessible to and supportive of all types of learners. Graphic organizers have become increasingly prevalent at schools in recent years and come in many varieties with names like Spider Map, Network Tree, Fishbone Map, and an oldie, but goodie, the Venn Diagram. Each is best suited to organizing information of a particular type. Using graphic organizers is something that almost all of our teachers already had some experience with, which could be reinforced through a *Friday Focus* memo.

Show, Don't Tell

I once attended a writing workshop, conducted by the bestselling author, Robert Newton Peck, whose books include one that is commonly read at the middle or high school level, *A Day No Pigs Would Die*. Peck emphasized that great writers avoid *telling* the reader what is occurring, instead writing in such a way that *shows* the reader what is happening. Peck reiterated this point several times, closing with the advice, "Don't just say the fat lady screamed; bring her on and let her scream." Teaching, then, is much like writing. In addition to telling students what we want them to learn, we must also show them what it is they must learn. We can do this through demonstrations, experiments, modeling, and using graphic organizers. In a metaanalysis of research studies conducted on the effectiveness of graphic organizers, Moore and Readence (1984) found that graphic organizer use elevated students' levels of reading comprehension. They also found even greater gains in vocabulary knowledge for students who used graphic organizers to improve vocabulary knowledge. In using graphic organizers, they found that the point of implementation is a critical factor in determining the extent of learning improvement, finding that improved learning outcomes were reported to a greater extent when graphic organizers are introduced as a follow up activity to a reading task as opposed to being used as a prereading activity.

Graphic organizers come in many different forms. I mentioned just a few previously, each with a different purpose. The Spider Map can be used when the information relating to a main idea or theme does not fit into a hierarchy. On the other hand, when the student needs to organize a hierarchical set of information, reflecting super ordinate or subordinate elements, this task is made easier suing a Network Tree. The Fishbone Map I referenced earlier can be used when cause-and-effect relationships are complex and nonredundant (Hall & Strangman, 2002).

Another advantage of using graphic organizers—and conducting training of teachers on the effective use of them in the classroom—is that they can be applied in virtually every curriculum area. Although the majority of research studies have been conducted in the area of reading, graphic organizers can be easily applied to math, language arts, science, social studies, foreign language, and almost any other subject that might be taught in a school.

The Ninth Friday

The author of this week's *Friday Focus* is Randy Herrin, a first year administrator at our school when he wrote the following memo. I asked Randy to write the weekly focus for the letter G as we moved through our A to Z instructional journey. Randy begins by sharing some humorous, though real, insights into his own career as a young student, suggesting that had graphic organizers been used, he might have learned more than he did. Randy also offers three specific types of graphic organizers for teachers at the school to use. Within his original *Friday Focus*, Randy directed teachers to visit the school's network share drive to access these graphic organizers. As mentioned previously, this can be an effective method for enhancing the *Friday Focus* by offering additional resources for interested teachers without embedding these resources directly into the *Friday Focus* itself, making the memo too long or too unwieldy. Randy closes with a humorous graphic organizer, using a Venn Diagram to compare and contrast himself to his predecessor at our school, an administrator who moved on to a different school in our system. Although it is not included below, depicting in a visual way what both Randy and his predecessor shared in common—the traits of baldness and a bit of a paunch—was a clever and fun way to make his point!

Friday, October 10

G is for Graphic Organizer

Students learn over half of what they know from visual images.

— Mary Alice White, Teachers College
at Columbia University (1999)

Two weeks ago I went to my thirtieth high school reunion in Jackson, Mississippi. It was good to see old friends and how they had changed over the years. My wife and I had a great time even though I talked to some people I didn't remember (a large graduating class).

The reunion started me thinking about my school days. I was an average student who made average grades. From what I can remember, most of my teachers lectured, and I spent most of my time not listening very well. If my teachers used graphic organizers or visual aids, especially those used today, I don't remember them. So my questions to you are: (a) When you present information to your students verbally, how much of it do they retain? (b) If your students see *and* hear the information, do they have a better comprehension of the material?

As a former Social Studies teacher, I used to require students to bring in a current event article with a brief written summary. There were some great summaries and some not so great. Lee Anne Rice recently shared with our staff a document she created that allows a student to breakdown their article so that her students have a better understanding of what they are reading. I have asked her to include this on our school's share drive for others to use. Thank you, Lee Anne!

Lee Anne's organizer can be used in several classes, but what about something for assisting students with vocabulary? As a drama teacher, my students often copied words and their definitions from the whiteboard and were expected to be prepared for tests on these vocabulary words. The graphic organizer below allows students to become actively involved with the vocabulary on many different levels. You can offer students a chance to share their sentences, clues, or what the word isn't. This allows students to not only recognize the new words, but also understand them.

Word	Dictionary Definition	My Definition or Clue	What the Word Isn't	Sentence

As an in-school suspension supervisor, I hoped every day that students serving with me didn't ask me anything about math, an area of personal struggle! The organizer in the link below was developed by teachers at Chestnut Oaks Middle School in Sumter, South Carolina (2008), for students like me. They had students who could grasp math word problems and those who couldn't. I would have been in the "couldn't grasp" group. Try this in your class if you like by following the hyperlink: http://coms.sumter17.k12.sc.us/site_res_view_folder.aspx?id=d2274d4d-2e4e-4839-8edf-8b10cb4fca28.

Now last, but not least, is the ever popular Venn Diagram. This particular diagram is a compare/contrast of my predecessor at our school, the great Van Lewsader and the "new guy," yours truly. Enjoy and I hope it makes you smile!

The purpose of graphic organizers is to assist students with understanding the material being taught. There are a variety of organizers available for your use; limit the number you use to those that are most effective for your purposes. And just think, if my teachers had used these types of teaching aides, I might have made valedictorian! Would you believe salutatorian? Principal's honor role? Okay, my mom was just happy I graduated!

Happy teaching & learning to all;
have a great weekend,

Randy

10

Differentiated Instruction Practices

The Tenth Friday

The following *Friday Focus* is a companion piece to one that had been written three weeks earlier (see Chapter 7). Both of these writings address the topic of differentiated instruction (DI). In the previous memo, which I wrote and shared with teachers, I attempted simply to convey some basic understandings of DI including what, exactly, the term means and how we can accomplish the challenging goal of varying our instruction to meet the varying learning needs of all students. In the following *Friday Focus*, I called on a special education teacher at our school, Erin Tracy-Lambrecht, to write more deeply on the topic, sharing her insights and wisdom based on her own training and experience. At the time she wrote this, Erin played a key leadership role in our district's work relating to differentiation of instruction. In addition to serving on district-level committees focusing on this topic, she had a great deal of personal experience successfully differentiating instruction in her own classroom. Because her students exhibited an extremely wide range of significant learning disabilities, Erin had—out of necessity—consistently planned and implemented ways to differentiate the content, process, product, and learning environment for them. As a teacher who was respected by her colleagues, I knew that her words would have an impact at our school and help to accomplish our goal of cultivating a school culture in which *all* teachers recognized the need to differentiate their instruction to meet the needs of *all* students.

Exemplary teachers do not use scripted, "one-size-fits-all" instructional lessons, resources, or styles. They realize that they are teaching students, not programs. The curriculum standards that must be learned are, obviously, of paramount importance, but exemplary teachers know that there are a variety of ways to teach the standards so that they optimize the likelihood that all students master them. Outstanding teachers not only recognize these individual differences in the students they teach, but embrace them, adjusting their practice accordingly. Most teachers in schools I have visited are willing to practice effective DI strategies, but not all of these willing teachers really know what differentiation is and what it is not. Earl (2003) touches on this in the following:

> Differentiation doesn't mean a different program for each student in the class, and it doesn't mean ability grouping to reduce the differences. It means using what you know about learning and about each student to improve your teaching so that students all work in ways that have an optimal effect on their learning. (p. 87).

In the following *Friday Focus*, Erin Tracy-Lambrecht elaborates on what DI is by offering specific ways that teachers in the school can differentiate the content, process, product, and learning environment in their classrooms. In addition, she offers ways that a few teachers in the school were already doing this, calling these examples *Eagle Ideas*, a reference to our school mascot. This became a neat feature of future *Friday Focus* writings as I, and others, would often highlight best practices we saw occurring in the school and share these as *Eagle Ideas* in our *Friday Focus* writings. Erin also showed how DI meshed logically with the work we were doing in our professional learning communities (PLCs). Finally, at the end of her *Friday Focus*, Erin added something that many past and subsequent *Friday Focus* authors included—a solid resource for those teachers wanting additional information and support relating to the *Friday Focus* topic.

Friday Focus

Friday, October 17

If a man does not keep pace with his companions, perhaps it is because he hears a different drummer.

— Henry David Thoreau

I have been fortunate to play a role in differentiation at various levels in our building. I continue to be impressed by the level of commitment, dedication, and passion that I see every day at our school. I consider our staff to be rich in resources with each other's knowledge and experiences. Differentiated instruction (DI) can be challenging and does require team effort and support. Ideally, this is a collaborative process between team members. I am including examples of how we are already differentiating for our students (*Eagle Ideas*) and what we can do to continue this process. I am writing this *Friday Focus* to generate student-centered discussions and ideas within our teams.

Differentiate the Content

One of the first steps we want to take in differentiating our content is to implement some sort of common assessment as a means of checking for previous knowledge. Before determining how to go about preassessing our students, there are three critical questions we must consider in shaping our framework for each unit. They are:

1. What is it we want our students to learn?

2. How will we differentiate according to the needs of our students?

3. How will we know when each student has learned it?

To gauge where our students stand, we must understand at which point they are starting. Giving an assessment can be as formal or informal as your team would like. For instance, teachers could implement a five-minute questionnaire based on the information in the text. The questionnaire could be given on paper (students respond in written form) or orally (students respond verbally). Once teachers have a better understanding of their students' abilities, they can then differentiate the content of that particular chapter.

☑ **Eagle Idea**

Sometimes, different versions of the same book for poorer readers; for some units that are thematically based, kids read different books.

— 8th Grade English

Differentiate the Process

Differentiating the process seems to happen naturally in our classrooms at Edgewood. When using graphic organizers to help focus our writing ideas, using charts to show differences among groups, using manipulatives in labs, and technology to incorporate our different learning styles, we are differentiating the process of how our students learn best.

☑ **Eagle Idea**

To differentiate in my math class, I use the overhead with notes for kids to copy and I verbally go through each piece. I also give copies of notes to students who I feel would benefit from not having to write down all information. I always write things down *and* verbally say them for kids who learn better visually or through auditory processing.

— 8th Grade Math

Differentiate the Product

After teachers have implemented the preassessment questionnaire, determining at which levels students are, they can determine how to differentiate the product. At this point, the team should revisit the questions: What is it that we want our students to learn? How will we know that they have learned it? Mastery of new concepts can be demonstrated in numerous ways. The team should consider how students who are at various learning levels can demonstrate mastery. One of my favorite units in sixth grade is when our students get to demonstrate their knowledge in both a one-page written response and a presentation on the Egyptian Unit. Within this product, Jason (sixth grade Social Studies) has modified the length of the written work, provided more emphasis on the presentation, and allowed for complete autonomy in the creative process (e.g., video presentation, game show etc.). This is a good example of how differentiating according to product can impact our students.

☑ Eagle Idea

In P.E., we grade our students based on the amount of push-ups they can complete. For our students who struggle, they are given the opportunity to do pushups using their knees. This way, they are still getting a good workout, but maintaining a style that is most comfortable for them.

— P.E. Dept.

Differentiate the Learning Environment

The process of learning, as we know, starts from the moment our students walk into our classrooms. If we believe that students learn in different ways, then we must consider the importance of creating a classroom environment that is conducive to those various learning styles. In differentiating, we should consider lighting, music, movement, and technology. Recently, I walked past the classrooms of Hal and Joanne (seventh grade Social Studies) where they were teaching a lesson on geography. The lights were turned off; the kids were on two sides, separated by hanging sheets. In a later conversation with Joanne, she explained to me that both she and Hal met to discuss a creative way to teach geography. I witnessed a human version of "battleship." This was a fantastic example of differentiating the environment using lighting and movement.

☑ Eagle Idea

I give students the opportunity to work in small groups and encourage peer correction to support the various levels in math. Depending on the day, I provide music for my students while they are working. I also allow students to work in the courtyard.

— 6th Grade Math

We will focus on DI at our Institute Day in November. In the meantime, I ask that you reflect and consider which one of these four areas of DI can be a focus for you, working as a team or a department. When we use each other to consider "the big picture," we are often able to share our ideas and gain support through the process. Continued good luck in working with your teams and a heartfelt thank you for the tireless hours you devote to each lesson to maximize the likelihood that each child reaches his or her full potential!

Enjoy your weekend!

Erin T.

PS: This is a wonderful website to use for support! Differentiated Instruction Help for Educators (2008): http://www.internet4classrooms.com/di.htm

11

Lesson Closure

Back to Basics

Every so often in the *Friday Focus*, I will write about something related to teaching and learning that is of a fairly mundane nature. These "back-to-basics" Friday memos usually result when I have noticed something occurring—or not occurring—in more than one classroom on a consistent basis. They usually focus on some aspect of teaching that we all know we should do but for a variety of reasons have gotten away from doing. For example, most schools are staffed with teachers who have learned a variety of designs for planning effective lessons. Although no teacher at any school in which I have worked really needed to be taught the basics of sound lesson design, I have observed many teachers who *know* each component of an effective lesson, but do not always *practice and implement* each of these elements. The "back to basics" *Friday Focus* memos are designed to enact immediate change in teaching practice in an area that is not overly complicated. In my experience, the most overlooked aspect of lesson design and implementation is that of lesson closure, which is something that can be addressed rather simply.

I would guess that the primary reason teachers do not consistently plan for and include an effective closing to each lesson they teach is related to time. They may have planned an effective closing to the lesson and simply ran out of time before getting to it or they did not plan for a closing at all due to everything else they wanted to squeeze into the lesson. Although many schools have adopted some form of block scheduling, allowing more time for each lesson, at the time of this *Friday Focus* writing, I was serving in a school at which teachers had only forty-one minutes of instructional time allotted for each class. As a result of these extremely short class periods, something vitally important to student learning—an effective lesson closure—was often missing from the lessons I observed.

Lesson closure can and should be a quick review to remind students what they have learned and to assist in planning the next lesson(s). Rick Smith (2004) identifies closure as the last three minutes of the lesson, which can be the most significant time of the entire lesson. Effective closure techniques can help teachers determine if additional practice is needed, if they need to reteach, or if they can move on to the next part of the lesson, unit, or concept. Closure is the final time to monitor student progress before moving on to the next learning objective. It is not enough to say, "Are there any questions?" as students begin gathering materials and tuning out. Teachers must plan for specific closing activities in order to maximize student learning. Lesson designs that have weak—or nonexistent—closure rob students of a critically important part of the lesson: an opportunity for them to think about, write about, discuss, show, etc., what they have learned. This time of student reflection allows students to internalize the skills that have been taught. In general, lesson closure will take anywhere from two to eight minutes and is most effective when it actively engages students in reflecting on the day's lesson. According to Pollock (2007), many teachers misunderstand closure and use it—if they use it at all—to restate in their own words what they have taught in the lesson. If teachers settle for summarizing the learning themselves, they get the benefit of the closure, not the students. Far better, then, to get students actively engaged in "closing" the lesson.

The Eleventh Friday

Writing about lesson closure falls under the category of what I have come to think of as a "back-to-basics" *Friday Focus* memo, relating to those key tenets of teaching we sometimes overlook and of which we need to be reminded periodically. In the following *Friday Focus*, I remind teachers about the importance of planning for and implementing closure activities on a consistent basis. I use an idea shared in the previous *Friday Focus* ("Eagle Ideas") to promote a few specific and effective closure activities I had observed during the school year in several classrooms. In this type of *Friday Focus*, I am simply reminding teachers of something they already know is important and trying to offer a few simple and specific ways to accomplish this important aspect of teaching. In some ways, these *Friday Focus* writings are the most popular with teachers, who usually responded by thanking me for sharing new, practical, and specific techniques that they could try out in their classrooms almost immediately.

Friday Focus!

Friday, October 24

Lesson designs that have weak closure rob students of the most important part of the lesson—the time when they have the opportunity to think about and discuss what they have learned. This is the time in the lesson when student reflection is necessary for internalization of the skills learned.

— Wolf & Supon, 1994

Obviously, the concept of lesson closure is not a new one to any teacher at our school. Yet I agree with the authors that it is a very important component of any effective lesson, and I fear that we often overlook it—mostly because of a lack of time. Instead, we merely conclude the lesson by assigning homework or preparing for dismissal. Closure—what the teacher does to bring the lesson to an appropriate or logical conclusion by giving the learner an opportunity to bring together the things they have just learned—is an essential component of lesson planning and student learning.

Although we typically think of closure as occurring at the end of a lesson, in actuality it can occur at any time throughout the lesson when the teacher wishes to clarify key points and ensure that students have understood the intended learning objectives. Whenever it is used, closure serves the purpose of summarizing main ideas, evaluating class processes, making decisions regarding questions posed at the outset of the lesson, and providing a bridge between what has occurred and what will occur in future lessons. Used effectively, closure can help students know *what* they learned, *why* they learned it, and *how* it can be useful (Phillips, 1987).

During our regularly scheduled days, most teachers have only forty-one minutes of instructional time allotted to them per class period. With such a short amount of time, it is very easy to fall into the trap of "closing" a lesson or lesson component simply by asking if there are any questions and moving forward. Again, it is important to go beyond this in order to decide whether or not students have mastered the intended learning and to add further insight and/or context to the lesson. In last week's *Friday Focus*, I liked how Erin employed the "Eagle Idea" device to illustrate how differentiated instruction is already being accomplished in our school. I plan on stealing her good idea in future FFs, spotlighting specific practices I have noticed Edgewood teachers using which relate to the weekly topic. As a start, although I cannot recall with 100% accuracy in which classrooms I have observed the list of closure ideas below, I have seen most, if not all, of these effective closure techniques used already this year at our school:

1. Ticket out the door: a one- or two-question pass that students complete in a few minutes and hand to the teacher on the way out.

2. Go around the room asking each student to state one thing they learned that day.

3. 3–2–1: Students write three things they found interesting, two things they learned, and one thing they still have a question about.

4. 3-Whats: *What* did we learn today? So *what*? Now *what*?

5. One student interviews another about what was learned in the lesson.

6. Student assumes role of the teacher and presents a summary of the day's learning to the rest of class.

7. Students write a postcard to their parents about what they learned that day.

8. Students discuss how the lesson is relevant in their lives.

9. Students write in a journal two or three things they learned that day.

10. Stumping the Stars: Desks are turned so that both halves of the classroom face each other. One group asks the other group three questions about the lesson. Students get thirty seconds to answer. Reverse the teams. If a team cannot answer the question, they must research it and present the answer to the class the next day.

Effective closure activities allow students to reflect upon and actively think about what happens in class. At the same time, they enable teachers to assess *what students got and what they did not* in order to plan for future learning. Including purposeful closure activities when planning and implementing our lessons is another way that we *Teach with Passion!* at our school.

Happy Weekend

Jeff

12

A Collaborative Learning Culture

The Twelfth Friday

I wrote the following *Friday Focus* while serving as principal at Edgewood Middle School in Highland Park, Illinois. The school and the school district were just beginning to focus on teacher collaboration as a key means for ensuring a guaranteed and viable curriculum across all grade levels and all schools within the district. As part of this focus on teacher collaboration, the district was dedicating much of its professional development efforts and resources to learning about Professional Learning Communities (PLCs), which were first popularized by Rick DuFour and Robert Eaker (1998). I had just retired from a school that had implemented PLCs as its framework for school improvement and enjoyed a great deal of success in doing so. We found that the single most important key to success with our PLC work was the emphasis on teacher collaboration. Finding time for teachers who teach the same academic courses to come together to examine curriculum standards, plan instruction, and analyze results proved transformational in terms of creating a positive and productive school culture. I was hoping to realize a similar transformation at my new school and school district and had already spoken at some length about my experience with PLCs during our first few staff meetings. The *Friday Focus* below was intended to summarize the key concepts of PLCs and let teachers know where we currently were in terms of serving as an authentic PLC and what remained to be done if we were to truly transform our school culture into one marked by focused teacher collaboration dedicated to the betterment of student learning.

In a collaborative school culture, members of the school community work together consistently, strategically, and effectively and are guided by a common purpose. All members of the school community—most significantly teachers and administrators—are guided by a common mission and vision and work together to ensure that these statements become realities. Together, the members of the school community set short-term goals that, when achieved, will lead them toward the common vision. These professionals commit to meeting regularly to improve their teaching and—more importantly—their students' learning. They agree to respect each other, valuing differences, sharing their ideas, and learning from each other. Unfortunately, in my experience working with hundreds of schools, I have found that the number of schools that merely *talk* about functioning as a PLC vastly outnumbers those that truly *exist* as authentic PLCs. Planned, implemented, and monitored consistently over time, the PLC framework can serve as a vehicle for transforming a school's culture. However, if educators merely talk about "being a PLC" without acting in ways that embody the PLC concepts, more harm than good can result. In my new school setting, I wanted to move forward steadily, but carefully, in "becoming" a PLC. On the one hand, I wanted to jump in right away. On the other, I knew that we had to begin by building the foundation for becoming a PLC by examining our mission, vision, and values, as well as learning the key concepts of PLCs as first outlined by DuFour and Eaker (1998).

One key to existing as a true PLC is, of course, collaboration. As with most school programs, initiatives, and concepts, there are schools in which certain teachers or departments excel at collaboration and seem to thrive at working together to improve their practice and their students' performance. However, to truly transform the culture of the entire school community, such pockets of excellence are not enough; effective collaboration must permeate the entire school community. Glickman (1998) views schools marked by a culture of collaboration as the best way to build and sustain effective teaching and learning in schools. He suggests that in schools exhibiting such a culture, teachers are always questioning their practices, guiding one another, planning together, coordinating practices, discussing important issues relevant to their profession, and taking a significant role in the school's decision-making process. Although the value of teacher collaboration has become more publicized in recent years, as far back as 1985, Saphier and King recognized the value of a collaborative school culture, outlining twelve characteristics of such schools:

- Collegiality
- Experimentation
- High expectations
- Trust and confidence
- Tangible support
- Reaching out to a knowledge base
- Appreciation and recognition
- Caring, celebration, and humor
- Involvement in decision making
- Protection of what's important
- Honest, open communication
- Traditions

Although I focused on the nuts and bolts of what a PLC is in the following *Friday Focus*, I knew that PLCs were simply a vehicle for becoming a school that exhibited the characteristics outlined above. To become a school known for having a collaborative culture, we needed to start by learning what a collaborative culture really means and looks like and begin building the foundation for future progress toward becoming one.

Friday Focus!

Friday, October 31

Creating a collaborative culture is the single most important factor for successful school improvement initiatives and the first order of business for those seeking to enhance the effectiveness of their schools.

— Kenneth Eastwood and Karen Seashore Lewis (1992)

During our opening gathering on the first Institute Day in August, we learned a good bit about Professional Learning Communities (PLCs). Although the first few hours back to school are hardly the ideal time to absorb new learning of a substantive nature, I have long been a fervent advocate of PLCs and all that they can accomplish—provided the process is undertaken slowly, steadily, and with a commitment on the part of all teachers and administrators within the school. Subsequent to our initial in-service, our English teachers participated in a morning workshop to learn more about PLCs and how they might benefit all District 112 schools. In addition, at our own recent Leadership Team meeting, Matt and I gave a copy of a fairly recent PLC book by Dufour, DuFour, Eaker, and Many (2006) titled, *Learning By Doing: A Handbook for Professional Learning Communities at Work,* to each team leader. Although I have read this book before, I enjoyed rereading it recently, and have asked our team leaders to undertake the task of reading one chapter each week and discussing the reading during our biweekly meetings. I hope that between now and the end of January—when we complete our study of this book—your team leaders will share with you what they have learned about PLCs and their personal thoughts on whether this is a framework for school improvement which we should consider as we move forward at Edgewood and in all District 112 schools.

I suspect that most everyone at Edgewood is at least somewhat familiar with PLCs and the success and notoriety that nearby Stevenson High School achieved through their work as they began the PLC journey that has continued for well over a decade now. Perhaps the most important "thing" to remember when we consider embarking upon a similar journey is that PLCs are not a "thing" at all. The PLC concept is not a program in any aspect, but a way of consistently and systematically conducting our core business of teaching and learning. A school that is functioning as a true PLC embraces certain *areas of focus that become embedded into the school's culture.*

There are, of course, a plethora of books written on the topic of Professional Learning Communities, many of which extol the virtues of PLCs and how they have dramatically impacted student and teacher learning around the world. I would commend several of these books to you, but, for now, I did want to share with you an abbreviated overview, which you will likely recall from previous learning. I repeat the basic information here because it truly encapsulates the entire PLC framework. Put simply, PLCs are basically centered on four critical questions all educators should ask themselves within a culture that emphasizes three key behaviors. A true Professional Learning Community includes members who exhibit (a) a focus on learning, (b) a focus on results, and (c) a collaborative culture.

Within this cultural framework, teachers and administrators constantly ask themselves the following four questions:

1. What is it we want our kids to learn?

2. How will we know if they have learned it?

3. How will we respond when kids do not learn?

4. How will we respond when kids have already mastered the intended learning objectives?

In a nutshell, the above statements are really all there is to the PLC concept! Moreover, the above seven statements are the essence of effective schools staffed by dedicated teachers who do not settle for merely *teaching* the curriculum, but instead ensuring that kids are *learning* the intended curriculum. Earlier this year, Todd Whitaker reiterated what I have already stated on several occasions: there is really only one thing that makes a school great and that is having great teachers. We are blessed to have great teachers at our school, *great teachers who focus on learning, focus on results, and work collaboratively to ask and answer the four critical questions posed above.*

That our district is embarking upon the PLC journey in earnest should be good news to all teachers at Edgewood because we are already halfway there—the critical components of a PLC are already in place to a certain extent at every grade level and in every subject area. Working together to further our focus in these areas is one more way we can *Teach with Passion!* throughout the school year.

Happy Weekend

Jeff

13

The Heart of Coaching

The Thirteenth Friday

My previous book *Improving Your School One Week at a Time* (2006) included thirty-seven *Friday Focus* memos, all of which were written by me or another educator at the school where I served as principal. After the first two years of using the *Friday Focus* as a teaching and learning communication at our school, we made another slight change: we periodically asked people from outside our school to author and share a *Friday Focus* memo with our school community. Since then, we have had many "guest authors" agree to write and share a *Friday Focus* memo. Although we have an infinite capacity within our own school to write a *Friday Focus* each and every week for many years, it has been a rewarding twist having respected people from outside the school building add to our body of writings. Typically, the person asked to write the *Friday Focus* is honored to do so and takes it quite seriously, and our teachers enjoy reading the insights of these "guest authors," often replying via e-mail to let them know how much their words were appreciated. Since we began this practice, we have had *Friday Focus* contributions from many within our own district, including the superintendent, assistant superintendents, directors, principals from other schools, and even our PTA president. As much as I enjoy writing my own thoughts on most Fridays, I really appreciate seeing what others are anxious to share, and the teachers with whom I have worked seem to benefit from these writings as well.

The following *Friday Focus* was written by Dr. L. C. Evans, currently superintendent of Forsyth County Schools in Cumming, Georgia. At the time of this writing, he had just come to the district as superintendent of our large school district, moving from a very small district in a different region of the state. He was replacing a highly respected outgoing superintendent who was retiring after a long and successful career in education, all in our district. Dr. Evans—more commonly known as "Buster"—made an immediate positive impression on the teachers in our district as he began filling his predecessor's very large shoes. He made it a point to visit each of the district's thirty schools, speaking at faculty meetings and visiting classrooms. In these visits, he shared who he was as a person as much, if not more than, who he was as a superintendent. He clearly valued building positive relationships and writes of this in his memo below. He also references the concept and importance of coaching, both in the traditional sense (the impact high school coaches had on his life as a teenager and beyond) and in the realm of peer coaching (teachers, principals, and superintendents coaching each other to improve performance). I hesitated before asking our new superintendent to take time from his already hectic schedule to share a *Friday Focus* writing with our school, but, in hindsight, this was a beneficial act for him as well as us. Our teachers felt appreciated that he recognized the *Friday Focus* was a deeply engrained component of our school culture and was willing and eager to honor this cultural tradition by sharing his thoughts with us so early in his tenure as superintendent.

A final note on the procedure I use for our "guest" *Friday Focus* authors: Whenever I have a guest author scheduled for the week, I have them e-mail their writing to me on Thursday. I then forward this to the staff Friday morning, including a brief note introducing and thanking the writer as a preface to the memo itself.

Friday Focus!

Friday, November 14

I am honored to have the opportunity to share some of my thoughts in this week's *Friday Focus* (FF) for Otwell Middle School. I have actually been reading every edition of FF prior to joining Forsyth County Schools. I believe that this type of regular sharing helps to keep us professionally focused on what makes a difference in educating students. Hopefully, there will be something in my comments that contributes to this ongoing professional learning effort.

You may have heard me quote this saying already, but I believe it is a core principle in teaching and student learning: "People don't care how much you know until they know how much you care." The educator translation of this is "students don't care how much you know until they know you care about them." I sense very strongly that this is true with today's student, perhaps even to a greater extent than it was when I was a student in junior high school. These relationships in the educational setting are multifaceted, as we are in a "people business" in which we work not only with students, but also peers, parents, and the community.

My journey through childhood, adolescence, and adult life was sprinkled with individuals who provided evidence that they cared about me as a person. The relationship and influence that I held with my parents led me to make decisions that were supportive of school achievement. Teachers, coaches, and sponsors of co- and extracurricular activities also influenced me in positive and powerful ways. Two of my most influential teachers were Joe McDaniel and Alton Sharpe. Both of these men were teachers and coaches. Although it has been years since I have seen these men, I still remember that both Coach McDaniel and Coach Sharpe accepted me and showed a strong interest in me both when I was a student in school and then in later years. I think that sometimes educators underestimate their impact on students. This impact can keep students engaged in school and learning, guiding them into adulthood. One of the factors correlating to high school completion is how connected a student felt to adults while in middle school.

What application can we make from these "affective domain"-related musings? First, we must embrace the fact that relationships matter and do make a difference in student engagement. Our relationships with our peers matter, and how we establish relationships that are supportive of student learning truly matter to students and their willingness to engage in the learning process. For a number of years I have been involved with the coaching program for new superintendents through the Georgia School Superintendent's Association. As a result, my library of books on "coaching" has grown to more than I have read, but in Crane's *The Heart of Coaching* (2007), he offers a formula to guide our coaching dialogue based on the vowels of the alphabet:

A Awareness

E Experience

I Intention

O Ownership

U Understanding

William James stated, "The deepest principle in human nature is the craving to be appreciated." Although I clearly do have too little space in this writing to fully explore or develop the above formula, I do believe that those whom we teach, we also coach. If we can ever get to the U of understanding, we understand that our students (and colleagues) want to be appreciated. Stephen Covey's *7 Habits of Highly Effective People* (1989) includes the habit "seek first to understand and then to be understood." For those teachers who truly connect with our students to pave the way for mastery of learning, I would guess that your evaluation of the five words listed above find meaning for you as you reflect upon your relationship with students.

I will end with another quote that perhaps sums up my thoughts on the importance of relationships in effective educational practice: "Whether 30 years later anything happens will be because a teacher made a difference. That encounter takes on almost a spiritual dimension. The ripple of influence never stops."

Thank you for what you do for our students. You *do* make a difference. You *do* influence lives. You *do* influence the lives of people both *today*… and *30 years later*.

Have a Wonderful Weekend!

Buster

14

A Culture of Gratitude

The Fourteenth Friday

On several occasions throughout a typical school year—Thanksgiving, Winter Holidays, Spring Break—I use the Friday before to deviate just a bit from the *Friday Focus* norm and instead write more of a personalized memo related to the occasion. Below is an example of such a *Friday Focus*, which I sent to the staff at Edgewood Middle School on the Tuesday before we let out for Thanksgiving break (thus the quotation marks around "Friday"). The purpose of this *Friday Focus* was simply to thank teachers at the school for all the good work they had done already through just over one-quarter of the school year and to remind them of the far-reaching impact they would have on the young people they were currently teaching.

In closing the *Friday Focus* which follows, I, of course, express happy Thanksgiving wishes to everyone; I also mention "SLCs," an abbreviation for our student-led conferences, which would be occurring immediately upon our return from Thanksgiving break and which were a vital component of our school culture. During our student-led conferences, students reported to their advisory teacher, who facilitated a conference led primarily by the student, who would explain and show his or her parents examples of their learning thus far in the school year. Again, the primary intent of what follows is simply to express thanks to our teachers and to remind them of the importance of their work. Although very little contained in this memo applies directly to the science of teaching, it did help to shape and maintain our school's culture, a culture in which we take time to reflect, give thanks, and celebrate our good work.

"Friday" Focus!

Tuesday, November 18

Perhaps some of you know the Paul McCartney song about a father's wishes for his son (although just a few days ago, my middle school administrative colleagues chided me for being enough of a geezer to know every stage of McCartney's career—not sure if Matt even knew who McCartney is). It reminds me of the wishes we have for our students. At Edgewood, we have teachers who are immensely influential and important in the lives of their students. You are nearly as important to your students as are their own fathers and mothers. Each day, you reach out your hand to our students to help them and to "make things clear." Whether you are teaching a lesson about Mesopotamia, fractions, rhyme scheme, history, or life in general, the hand you reach out to your students each day will be remembered long after it is extended. Many of you have probably already heard of or read the story below, and I know it's just a little bit sappy, but I wanted to share it again as an apt expression of thanks for all that you, as teachers, do to help our students.

> Thanksgiving Day was near. The first grade teacher gave her class a fun assignment—to draw a picture of something for which they were thankful. Most of the class might be considered economically disadvantaged, but still many would celebrate the holiday with turkey and other traditional goodies of the season. These, the teacher thought, would be the subjects of most of her student's art. And they were.

> But Douglas made a different kind of picture. Douglas was a different kind of boy. He was the teacher's true child of misery, frail and unhappy. As other children played at recess, Douglas was likely to stand close by her side. One could only guess at the pain Douglas felt behind those sad eyes. Yes, his picture was different. When asked to draw a picture of something for which he was thankful, he drew a hand. Nothing else. Just an empty hand.

> His abstract image captured the imagination of his peers. Whose hand could it be? One child guessed it was the hand of a farmer, because farmers raise turkeys. Another suggested a police officer, because the police protect and care for people. Still others guessed it was the hand of God, for God feeds us. And so the discussion went—until the teacher almost forgot the young artist himself. When the children had gone on to other assignments, she paused at Douglas' desk, bent down, and asked him whose hand it was. The little boy looked away and murmured, "It's yours, teacher."

She recalled the times she had taken his hand and walked with him here or there, as she had the other students. How often had she said, "Take my hand, Douglas, we'll go outside." Or, "Let me show you how to hold your pencil." Or, "Let's do this together." Douglas was most thankful for his teacher's hand. Brushing aside a tear, she went on with her work.

Teachers, thank you for reaching out your hand each day to our kids here at Edgewood. While we have many students from affluent families with loving mothers and fathers, we also have our share of "Douglases." Your hand means a great deal to both. So often, when I visit your classrooms, I witness "first hand" the power of your hands, as students soak in your wisdom, your warmth, your passion. Many of our students express their appreciation immediately through their engagement, their quality work, and by returning your smiles with their own. Others are less obviously responding to the hand you tirelessly extend; yet they, too, are storing away these moments and will remember you and your steady hand long after they have left us. Sometimes we use our hands to applaud our students for an outstanding effort in the classroom or in an extracurricular activity. Other times, we use our hands to pray for those students who are especially on our minds. We also use our hands to greet our students each day, as we shake theirs, and wish them a happy day. Lending a helping hand in all its many variations is one way that we *Teach with Passion* each day! Give yourselves a "hand" for work well done each and every day, including your work preparing for our conferences next week. I know our parents and students are thankful as well.

Best Wishes for successful SLCs
and a Glorious Thanksgiving

Jeff

15

A Community of Leaders

In Chapter 3, I described how we modified the *Friday Focus* slightly nearly every year, focusing on teaching and learning issues confronting all educators, ranging from A to Z for the majority of our writings one year, and examining one of the twenty-seven school standards comprising the Georgia School Standards (GSS), which outlined specific actions successful schools plan, implement, and monitor another. In Chapters 3 and 4, I included *Friday Focus* writings from our third year, during which we examined one of these school standards. This chapter includes one more *Friday Focus* relating to the theme of school standards, focusing specifically on the area of leadership.

Everyone's a Leader

For many years, it seemed as if every school I visited proclaimed themselves—using words that varied only slightly from school to school—a "community of learners." Perhaps there can be no goal more apt and noble for a school than this; after all, our core business is certainly learning. Moreover, in today's rapidly changing society, it truly is the case that we must strive to inspire our young people to become lifelong learners, able to keep up with such rapid and incessant change. Although I respected those schools proclaiming to be bastions of learning for all, I was even more struck by a high school I visited at which the principal confided that—as much as he valued learning—he was even more keenly interested in creating a community of *leaders*. I listened as he explained that his goal was for every student and adult in the building to become a leader in some area. Some people, of course, held positions that inherently required they serve as leaders, from administrators to department chairs, to the football coach to the student body president. Yet, he took this a step further, challenging each incoming freshman student and each new teacher he hired to identify some area of interest, passion, or expertise they possessed and lead others in learning about or getting involved with their passion as well. After just a few years as principal at this large high school, he had visibly transformed the school's culture into one in which nearly every student and adult in the building was successfully and enthusiastically playing a leadership role in a specific area. Virtually every student in the large senior class mentored one or more underclassmen. The school secretary had a weekly "lunch bunch" she invited to her office to review academic progress or just to talk. The school custodian had taken over the primary leadership of students assigned to work detail around the campus for a variety of academic or behavioral infractions. Freshman students visited the feeder middle schools, meeting with and talking to eighth graders and helping them transition successfully to high school. A culture in which every member was expected to serve as a leader had clearly been achieved and I marveled at how much *learning* was occurring as a result of all this *leading*.

The most effective, intelligent, and hardworking principal alive today cannot lead a school alone and certainly cannot single-handedly dictate, change, create, or define the school's culture. This can only be accomplished through the collective efforts of a team of effective leaders. The larger the school, the more leaders are needed within that school to truly make a difference in shaping the culture of the school. Stated simply, school leadership—and, concomitantly, school improvement—must come from all members within the school community. As Roland Barth (1990) has stated, school leadership must be considered not only in terms of roles, but also in terms of functions:

> School leadership can come from principals who transform adversaries into colleagues; from teachers who individually take responsibility for the well-being of the school; from parents who translate a basic concern for their children into constructive actions; and from students who guide tours or in other ways offer community service (p.144).

The Fifteenth Friday

The following *Friday Focus* examines the second leadership standard contained in the Georgia School Standards (GSS). On the surface, Standard 2 focuses primarily on the leadership capabilities of the principal and other school administrators. However, in unpacking this school standard, it is clear that the kind of leadership required of school administrators is a type of leadership that actively engages every teacher in the school in some leadership role related to improving student and school performance. As a result, I begin the *Friday Focus* by explaining the goals that the administrative team held as school leaders, and follow up by challenging each staff member to also play a vital leadership role at our school, making their own visions a reality and improving our school in the process. I also reiterate what was a common refrain at this school and what we wanted to continue to emphasize as part of our school's culture: that we would learn together and lead together while working congenially *and* collegially.

Friday Focus!

Friday, November 28

No matter how good he is, no leader can do it alone. Just as a sports coach needs a team of good players to win, an organization needs a team of good leaders to succeed. The larger the organization, the stronger, larger, and deeper the team of leaders needs to be.

— John Maxwell (2002)

Leadership Standard 2 of the Georgia School Standards (GSS) reads as follows: *The principal and school administrators exhibit instructional leadership and serve as the lead learners.* A four-point rating rubric is offered ranging from "beginning" to "full" implementation with the following description characterizing *Full Implementation*: *The principal and school administrators exhibit a deep understanding of teaching and learning, which fosters focused, professional learning. Teachers are involved in data analysis, reviewing student work, and making decisions about instructional practices* (GDOE, 2008).

So, this is the standard and what full implementation looks like. Our task, then, is to determine where we currently are and what we need to do to reach the highest performance level possible. Obviously, as administrators at our school, Van, Beth, Suzanne, and I all strive to earn "full implementation" status in helping our school by serving as lead learners and lead teachers. We rely, however, on each teacher to carry out our school's core work in leadership: leading our students to become successful and lifelong learners themselves. In my opinion, two words are at the heart of what we try to do in the area of school leadership: *congeniality* and *collegiality*. These two words are often confused for each other. Used correctly, congeniality is often subordinated in importance to collegiality. I maintain that both are necessary for any school hoping to serve as a strong community of professional learners and leaders. We must certainly work in a spirit of *congeniality*—that is, we must enjoy each other's company and get along well with one another. I know that Van, Suzanne, Beth, and I enjoy each other's company and we laugh often together. We have also developed many close professional friendships with the teachers and support staff at our school. We take great joy in seeing this same spirit of congeniality among teams of teachers throughout the building. When I viewed the photo story that Doris created to accompany her own *Friday Focus* a few weeks back, I was struck by the number of smiling teacher faces that were included, so many of you enjoying each other's company. I am most thankful that we have a congenial staff. How miserable it would be to work this hard and not enjoy the companionship of those with whom we interact each day.

We also have established and must continue to cultivate an atmosphere of *collegiality*, which is vitally important if we are to continue learning and improving. Judith Warren Little (1982) suggests that collegiality in schools is marked by the presence of four specific behaviors:

1. Adults in the school talk about practice. These conversations about teaching and learning are frequent, continuous, concrete, and precise.

2. Adults in schools observe each other engaged in the practice of teaching and administration. These observations become the practice to reflect on and talk about.

3. Adults engage together in work on the curriculum by planning, designing, researching, and evaluating curriculum.

4. Adults in schools teach each other what they know about teaching, learning, and leading. Craft knowledge is revealed, articulated, and shared.

The above four behaviors are occurring with regularity in our school. In discussing where we are as leaders, we look at what all the adults in the building are engaged in as Little suggests. As adults, we are all leaders at our school and the way we begin to lead is by engaging in the activities described above.

Like many of you, I strive to be a reflective leader and learner, continuously examining my leadership behaviors and how I can improve. I often share with you Roland Barth's definition of a leader, which I first heard him share at the conference several of us attended: "making happen that which you believe in." I hold fast to many educational beliefs that, I hope, comprise an overall philosophy of leadership and schooling. We should all examine our individual and collective beliefs regarding our noble profession regularly, "clarifying our core values." I have even come to describe my own "CORE" educational values as an acronym: Communication, Observation, Relationships, and Expectations (2008). I try to incorporate these four core practices into the work we do here. Thank you for also examining your own core values—as a teacher and as a leader. Each of you leads our kids on a daily basis, but you also lead—and learn from—each other. A common thread between congeniality and collegiality, I think, is sharing. To establish *congeniality*, we share quite a bit about who we are as people. To establish *collegiality*, we share who we are as professionals. Thank you for serving as teachers who are also leaders, people who are always willing to share who you are and what you stand for. You have worked hard to help Van, Suzanne, Beth, and I as we strive to earn and maintain "full implementation" status on this important GSS standard. Remember Barth's definition of a leader: "making happen what you believe in." Doing this is one way that you *Teach and Lead with Passion* each day!

Happy Weekend!

Jeff

16

Making it Stick

Book Reviews

Periodically, I use the weekly *Friday Focus* communication to share with teachers something I have enjoyed learning through my professional reading. At times, of course, I am sharing something I have learned from reading works by Bob Marzano, Doug Reeves, Ron Clark, or some other well-known educator. Often, however, I try to find books that relate to the world of education but were not necessarily intended for an audience of teachers. Several books originally written for the business sector subsequently became quite popular fodder for book studies in schools and school systems. Perhaps the most obvious example is Jim Collins's well-known *Good to Great: Why Some Companies Make the Leap…and Others Don't* (2001). In my first book, *Improving Your School One Week at a Time* (2006), I included a *Friday Focus* memo I had written about Collins' book. Originally intended for corporate organizations, *Good to Great* also resonated with school leaders, many of whom ordered copies for the purpose of conducting book studies with teachers and administrators in their schools or school districts. Largely because of the success of this book with educators across the country, Collins published a monograph to accompany *Good to Great* in 2005 called *Good to Great and the Social Sectors.*

Over the years, I have written about a dozen *Friday Focus* memos that were, in essence, book reviews. These *Friday Focus* writings consisted of my thoughts on a book I had read that I believed could in some way translate to our teaching practices in classrooms. Many teachers seemed to enjoy these "book review" *Friday Focus* memos; each time I shared such a *Friday Focus*, several teachers told me they went out to purchase the book being reviewed so they could read the entire thing. The importance of reading professional literature directly related to the world of teaching and learning should be a given for all who consider themselves professional educators. However, I have found it equally important to keep up with—and share with staff—professional literature relating to the corporate world. Corporations and school systems differ dramatically in a number of ways. However, successful, high-performing companies have much in common with successful, high-performing schools. First and foremost is a positive workplace culture.

I have long maintained that the corporate world can learn a great deal about how to improve the corporate workplace by examining successful schools. The inverse is equally true: There is much we, as educators, can learn from the corporate world that will help our students and our schools thrive. Although dramatic differences exist between the two, building and maintaining a positive workplace culture that enhances organizational effectiveness and efficiency is a trademark of excellence in both high-performing schools and high-performing corporations.

Of the dozen or so *Friday Focus* "book reviews" I have written and shared over the years, the following five titles (in addition to *Good to Great* and Thomas Friedman's *The World is Flat: A Brief History of the 21st Century* (2006), which I write about in Chapter 26) are ones I find most helpful to teachers and teacher-leaders striving to improve teacher effectiveness, school leadership, or school culture:

- *Stupid, Ugly, Unlucky, and Rich: What Really Leads to Success* (2005) by Richard St. John

- *The Knowing-Doing Gap: How Smart Companies Turn Knowledge into Action* (2000) by Jeffrey Pfeffer and Robert I. Sutton

- *The Five Dysfunctions of a Team: A Leadership Fable* (2002) by Patrick Lencioni

- *Wikinomics: How Mass Collaboration Changes Everything* (2008) by Don Tapscott and Anthony D. Williams

- The Leadership Challenge (2008) by James M. Kouzes and Barry Z. Posner

Although none of the above books were written for or by public school educators, each contains valuable information which can help us become better teachers and better teacher leaders.

The Sixteenth Friday

The following is example of a "book review" *Friday Focus* written about the bestselling book, *Made to Stick: Why Some Ideas Survive and Others Die* (2007) by brothers and coauthors Chip and Dan Heath. This book is one of my all-time favorite examples of a book not originally intended for teachers, yet so meaningful to teachers—in particular those who want to increase the likelihood that their students will retain the information they are imparting. Like *Good to Great,* this book became so popular with educators that the Heaths subsequently published an article based on the book, but specifically geared to teachers, called *Teaching That Sticks* (2007). The *Friday Focus* memo below very briefly outlines six characteristics that increase the likelihood that messages will be more readily retained by an audience. In schools, of course, our primary audience includes every student in every classroom. If we can learn how to deliver our messages in ways that are more likely to be well received by our students, we are improving student learning and, therefore, our teaching. I have found that the six key qualities that help ideas stick in the "real world" are also qualities that help ideas stick in the classroom. After talking about these qualities in a faculty meeting and sending out this *Friday Focus*, many teachers began sharing among themselves new strategies they were trying to make their lessons "stick" with their students.

Friday Focus!

Friday, December 5

And that's the great thing about the world of ideas—any of us, with the right insight and the right message, can make an idea stick....For an idea to stick, it's got to make the audience: (1) pay attention; (2) understand and remember it; (3) agree/believe; (4) care; (5) be able to act on it.

— Chip & Dan Heath (2007a)

At a recent faculty meeting, I spent a few minutes sharing some ideas I gleaned from reading the excellent book referenced above. Although this book was not written specifically for educators, it did include many examples about teachers and how the best teachers get students to learn material in a way that "sticks" with them over time. The authors offer six principles for successfully communicating ideas, which seem so relevant to classroom instruction. These six strategies for making ideas stick can be compacted into the acronym SUCCESs to represent:

- **Simple:** The authors suggest that if you say three things, you don't say anything. They advocate stripping an idea down to its very core, relentlessly prioritizing what it is we want to communicate. Yet, brevity alone will not work; the idea of communicating in proverbs is ideal: creating ideas that are both simple *and* profound. Think of how this applies to teaching our students. So often, less is more, in that our students will latch on to simple, but powerful, messages.

- **Unexpected:** Our kids tend to pay attention more when we present material in unexpected ways. The authors recommend "breaking a pattern" when desiring to make ideas stick. We must generate interest and curiosity by systematically "opening gaps" in our students' knowledge and then setting about "filling those gaps."

- **Concrete:** We make our ideas more clear to others, causing them to understand and remember, when we consider the principle of concreteness. We must explain our ideas in terms of human action and sensory information. Abstract truths can be made concrete, for example, in widely known sayings such as "a bird in hand is worth two in the bush." Speaking concretely is the only way to ensure that our ideas will mean the same thing to everyone in our audience.

- **Credible:** Our students will believe what we say and/or agree with us when we implement the principle of credibility. When we try to build a case for something, most of us instinctively reach for hard data. But in most cases, this is exactly the wrong approach. The authors use the example of Ronald Reagan's message in defeating Jimmy Carter. He could have cited innumerable statistics regarding the economy, but instead asked a simple question: "Before you vote, ask yourself if you are better off today than you were four years ago."

- **Emotions:** We can encourage students to care about what we are saying and trying to teach through emotions. That is, we must make them *feel* something. The authors invoke what they call the "Mother Teresa principle," which is: "If I look at the one, I will act," meaning that it may be easy to overlook problems on a large scale until we put an individual human face on the problem—when we know one person suffering from the problem, we are more likely motivated to act. The authors suggest cultivating a sense of caring within others through the power of association and appealing to others' self-interest and identity.

- **Stories:** We get others to act on our ideas through the use of effective storytelling. Hearing stories prepares us to respond more quickly and effectively. Certainly, in the classroom, many of you are masters at disguising lectures as page-turning stories that our kids recall with clarity. Stories can be used as stimulation (telling people how to act) and inspiration (giving people energy to act). The authors believe in using three different types of stories for three different purposes: (1) Challenge Stories (to overcome obstacles); (2) Connection Stories (to get along or reconnect); and (3) Creativity Stories (to inspire a new way of thinking).

Obviously, it is of paramount importance that we, as teachers, get our curriculum standards "to stick" with our students. I found the authors' SUCCESs framework for making ideas in the "real world" stick to be equally applicable to the classroom setting. To help our students retain the messages we are communicating, we need to keep it simple and include the unexpected. We need to make our presentations concrete and credible. We need to use the power of emotions and storytelling. What wonderful ways to present information to adolescents so that they will feel compelled to pay attention, understand, believe, care, and act.

In reading this book, I thought of many teachers at our school who excel in one or more of the above areas of communicating information to others. The authors could have used our school for all the examples they wanted to include for each of the six principles. We have worked hard to identify with precision and clarity just *what* it is we want our kids to know. Making this information stick with our kids can be challenging at times, but by considering the SUCCESs principles, we increase the likelihood that students will remember core curriculum material. Doing this is another way that we *Teach with Passion* each day!

Happy Weekend!

Jeff

17

Teaching Organization Skills

Study Skills for Student Success

It seems as if some educators start complaining that their students do not possess or exhibit any study skills at about the Kindergarten level and continue to bemoan the lack of these skills all the way through grade 12, and even beyond. In many cases, it is quite true that students in grades K–12 are lacking the study skills they need to achieve at optimal levels of performance. However, too often, complaining about how our students do not possess these skills is about as far as we go as educators. To really make a change in our schools and a difference in the lives of our students who seemingly do not know how to study, we need to provide direct instruction in the area of study skills. In addition to teaching study skills at all grade levels in our elementary schools, I recommend that all students be required to complete a course focusing on study skills as part of their transition to both middle school and high school. What we require of students each time they leave one level of schooling and move to another changes dramatically. It is important that we begin this process of change by explicitly teaching what will be required of students for them to succeed as learners.

In one school where I served as principal, all students were offered the opportunity to take French or Spanish all three years. However, although the foreign language class met daily at grades 7 and 8, it convened only every other day at the sixth grade level. On alternate days, all sixth grade students were enrolled in a "student skills" class. We found this to be a realistic model for teaching study skills as students entered the middle grades years. At a high school where I served as an assistant principal, we took a slightly different approach while still requiring every incoming freshman student to complete a study skills course. For the first quarter of the school year, all freshman students were enrolled in a study skills class in place of a different elective (health, PE, art, etc.) which they would then pick up during the second quarter. Again, the intent was to make certain we provided all incoming students with direct instruction related to the skills they would need to possess as successful learners at the high school level. Although these classes were seldom students' favorite classes, I can say that many students benefited a great deal from them and even came to realize this for themselves as they progressed through their middle or high school years.

Providing direct instruction in the area of "study skills" can encompass a wide array of topics. One program I have seen used for teaching student skills was developed by Archer and Gleason (1993). This research-based program provides for direct instruction of study skills students will use across the curriculum, including six key areas:

- School behavior and organization skills
- Learning strategies
- Strategies for studying for and taking tests
- Textbook reference skills
- Reading and interpreting graphs
- Dictionary and encyclopedia reference skills

By explicitly teaching the above skills—particularly at critical times in our students' educational careers—we enhance the likelihood that they will learn more in the areas we are truly passionate about, from reading and writing to technology and music.

The Seventeenth Friday

The following *Friday Focus* was written by Dr. Rachel Cohen, who served as a Behavior Intervention Specialist and School Psychologist at Edgewood Middle School in Highland Park, Illinois. As noted above, there are many topics that can fall under the broad category of "student skills." In this particular memo, Rachel focuses primarily on one aspect of such skills, which is using—effectively—an assignment notebook. Such notebooks exist in almost all schools and they come in a wide variety of shapes, colors, sizes, and even names. Some schools call them agenda books, student handbooks, organizers, or planners. Regardless of the name, size, or style, such organizers can be useful tools for our students and for us—*if* we take the time to teach our students how to use them and monitor their usage periodically. Student assignment notebooks can help our kids learn time management skills, keeping track of homework assignments, projects, and tests. Teachers who take the time to explicitly teach proper use of assignment notebooks may actually save instructional time in the process, as Dr. Cohen points out below. Anytime we teach a procedure of any type, it does take away from instructional time—but only in the short term. The more we teach such procedures up front, the better our students become at following them as the year progresses and the less time we will have to spend on such procedural stuff on the back end.

In Rachel's *Friday Focus*, she notes that her writing is part one of what was a two-part *Friday Focus*. Although it is not included in this book, two of our school's social workers wrote the next *Friday Focus* on study habits and concentrated on breaking down large-scale assignments into smaller parts. Rachel describes the student skills instruction in place at our school in the sixth grade and cites much of the research associated with the program we used, *Advanced Skills for School Success* (Curriculum Associates, 2009). She also shares how she and others at our school had worked during lunch periods to help some of our seventh and eighth grade students who needed extra support in the area of organization. Finally, she closes with more "Eagle Ideas" from teachers throughout the school who were directly teaching organization in some way to the students they taught.

Friday Focus!

Friday, December 12

If it weren't for the last minute, nothing would ever get done.
— Author Unknown

As I finish writing this *Friday Focus* on Thursday, I know this quote certainly applies to me. I wonder how many of you could relate to it as well. But, I did write down the tasks to complete this FF in my planner. Monday, I noted to e-mail teachers for "Eagle Idea" tips. Tuesday, I noted that I would stay late to work on this. Friday, I noted that it was due. I am telling you this because the topic of this FF is using the assignment notebook to develop good habits to plan, organize, and complete work. This is a two-part series. I will focus on the use of the assignment notebook; in a subsequent *Friday Focus*, Meghan and Brittany will emphasize breaking down long-term projects.

As many of you know, Brittany, Meghan, and I have spent the past six weeks working with eighteen organizationally challenged students and their parents in a study skills intervention. We implemented the *Advanced Skills for School Success* curriculum, a sixty-lesson curriculum focused on organization, test taking, note taking, and participating in class. This is the same curriculum that our student skills teachers are now using in the sixth grade student skills class. Many parents of these seventh and eighth graders suggested that we teach this same curriculum in sixth grade—it was nice to be able to tell them that we were!

This curriculum was carefully developed through the input of more than 500 middle school teachers. Researchers (Archer & Gleason, 1993) studied schools that were implementing this curriculum and found that the *proper use of the assignment notebook* alone made a huge difference. When students *brought* their *assignment notebooks* to class, they were *more likely* to also *bring a pen, pencil, and piece of paper* (*94%* of the students vs. only *62%* without a notebook). Research also found that when students *recorded homework* in their assignment notebook, they were more likely to *return their homework*! Finally, *four minutes* of class time was saved when students *used assignment notebooks* because they were able to *locate papers* or assignments more quickly in response to teacher directions. Therefore, while using and reviewing the assignment notebook may seem like it takes additional class time, it actually *saves class time*.

To reinforce these practices in our study skills groups, we first set up a system in which students were accountable for independently coming to the group and bringing their pen/pencil, binder, and assignment notebook. We checked each week to make sure students had each item. We noted this on a chart. If they brought *everything*, we gave them a reward, as simple as a pen, pencil, or highlighter. Believe it or not, they actually got excited about this. It could also be because we made a really big deal about it. And nearly every student brought nearly everything each week. That's quite an accomplishment for the organizationally challenged. We know that you cannot provide rewards or prizes for all of your students each day, but you could incorporate other fun and free reinforcers, such as a few minutes of free time.

Once the students were prepared, the first lesson was on abbreviations for the assignment notebook. With such a small space provided, it is important that students can write in all the information they need. We checked each week to make sure they were using the abbreviations we taught them. The hardest one for them was ¶, but they finally got it. We practiced using these abbreviations each week, too. Next, we taught them how to use the monthly calendar. I bet most students at Edgewood do not even use their monthly calendar! The seventh graders really liked using the monthly calendar (the eighth graders grumbled a bit more). They liked to see the big picture, just like teams use the big calendars in the hallway. They also found that it served as an extra reminder. Finally, we taught them the importance of writing down projects and tests on the *due date*. Then, they are able to go back and plan what they need to do each day. Overall, we found the most helpful ingredient was the weekly checking of the assignment notebooks. One student titled this checking as "nagging," but he did admit that it helped!

Now that we won't be meeting with the students on a weekly basis, we need your help to maintain these skills, especially the use of the assignment notebook. I know many of you remind students to write down assignments in their assignment notebooks each day. I also know that many of you sign and check assignment notebooks. Regular and random checks do increase the use of the assignment notebook. We found this out as we gradually saw more and more entries written in the students' assignment notebooks over the course of the six weeks. In closing, I will share what some teachers at our school are doing in their classrooms to emphasize organization. How many of these do you do every day or week?

☑ **Eagle Ideas**

- Every Monday, Todd does a "week at a glance" where he previews all the assignments and due dates for the week. At this time, he has students take out their assignment notebooks and write everything down.

- Every day, Elaine asks students to take out their assignment notebook to review short- and long-term projects coming up. She asks students to tell her what is on the agenda to ensure that they are aware of all the upcoming assignments. This way, she knows that they know!

- Every day, Carly writes the assignments on one place of the board. She tells the students to get out their assignment notebook and write the assignment down. Sound familiar?

- Lindsay has one class in which the students tend to be forgetful and put less effort into their homework than other classes. She wants them to understand the importance of daily rehearsal. She takes ten minutes *every* day at the end of class to go over daily, weekly, and long-term assignments. Like Elaine, she makes the class repeat certain items aloud, so the next day when a student says, "You did not say that," or "I do not remember that," she can say, "Remember, we said it out loud together!" The other students tell the other ones the same thing! She also writes the assignments on the homework board, under the daily agenda, on her website, and long-term assignments are found on her team's calendar. To do a check on some students without drawing attention to them, she will check *all* notebooks. Some days, she even stamps the notebooks. She said it is like being back in first grade, and they love it!

- Other teachers give assignment notebook quizzes. For example, a teacher will say, "Look at October 27th. Write down the math assignment from that day." Students can earn an incentive for having the correct answer. If a student does not have their assignment notebook, they lose out.

In conclusion…you may be wondering, did study skills work? I guess you will be the judge of that. As one student said, "It wasn't that I didn't know these skills, I just wasn't using them. I just needed to be reminded." Thanks to all teachers for "reminding students" to use these positive habits each and every day!

Rachel

18

A Culture of Giving

The Eighteenth Friday

The following *Friday Focus* is one that I wrote on the final Friday before our winter holiday break. On one level, it is simply a personal reflection I shared with teachers about my father, who had passed away just a year before after an unpleasant battle with pancreatic cancer. Yet, in reflecting on my father just prior to what would be my family's first Christmas holiday without him present, I was also sharing with teachers what made my dad a great teacher—many of the same traits that the teachers at this school possessed and which I wanted to acknowledge. As I mention in the writing below, my father was a business executive who knew almost nothing of the education profession. At the same time, he innately lived his life as a teacher and I hoped that some of his natural tendencies in this area would be ones that "real" teachers could learn from.

As I write each *Friday Focus*, I like to think, of course, that all teachers in the school are reading them, learning from them, and enjoying them. From discussions I have had with these teachers—both in person and via e-mail exchanges after the *Friday Focus* is distributed—it is clear that, at the very least, on *most* Fridays, *most* teachers take the time to read and reflect on whatever is included in the *Friday Focus*. I must say that, although I receive responses to every *Friday Focus* memo that goes out, it seems as if the percentage of responses increases on those occasions when I am writing from a more personal approach, such as the writing that follows. Specifically, I recall receiving many e-mails from teachers at our school shortly after sending out this particular version of the *Friday Focus*. Of course, this may simply be the case because such *Friday Focus* memos are the exception rather than the norm, but I believe that in schools with positive school cultures, the adults are not unlike the kids in that they want to know how much you care before they care how much you know. When I sent the following *Friday Focus*, I was serving as principal with teachers who knew almost everything about me as a professional and as a person. In kind, I made it a point to know as much as I could about their families and circumstances. I knew that the teachers at this school cared about me as a person; I wanted them to know that I cared about them as individuals, too. Because almost all the adults in the building cared about each other as people, our culture was one in which professional collaboration and sharing was expected and embraced.

On a final note, it is obvious from the *Friday Focus* below that writing about the Christmas holiday was an acceptable and even welcome part of the school's culture. Of course, this very same writing would not be appropriate in all schools and it almost goes without saying that we must understand the community in which we serve, respecting all races, religions, and holiday traditions. Shortly after leaving this school, I served in a school at which very few of the students observed Christmas as a holiday; thus it would have been inappropriate to share such sentiments in that setting. Yet, I still would find a way to share the more important—and personal—aspects of the message below, even if I felt it inappropriate to include holiday references of any kind. In schools with positive cultures, the idea of giving—in all its meanings—is widely embraced as a core component of why we do what we do. Teachers give of themselves to their students each day in their classrooms. Educators must also give to each other. We must give what we know, what we stand for, what we care about—and who we are.

Friday Focus!

Friday, December 19

We make a living by what we get, but we make a life by what we give.
— Winston Churchill

Happy, happy Christmas, that can win us back to the delusions of our childhood days, recall to the old man the pleasure of his youth, and transport the traveler back to his own fireside and quiet home!
— Charles Dickens

Although the Christmas season remains my absolute favorite time of year, I confess that the current one is just a tad bittersweet, because it will be the first I've spent without one of my best friends, my dad, who passed away this October. He was a pretty cool guy who managed to achieve the perfect balance described above by Churchill, of making a living and making a life through his work and his giving. He made a living primarily through forty-three years of employment with Kraft Foods. He made a life by giving freely of his time, money, love, laughter, and shrewd advice to friends, coworkers, and family.

Like other teachers at Otwell, presumably, I would say that my father was the best teacher I ever had. As a businessman, he knew very little about the education profession, and even held some rather archaic views about our chosen career (e.g., because he spoke no English himself until he began school in Chicago at age six, he felt that all children today should simply be thrown into the mix and expected to learn English as he did). Yet, he intuitively knew how to motivate young people. Although he did this in many ways, a primary one that still strikes me was his unwavering inclination to *identify young people's strengths and interests and build off them*. Any interest of mine as a youngster seemed to immediately become a passion of his. Throughout my life, whenever he met any of my friends, he did the same with them. I recall a business trip that required that he fly to New York City, from our home in Chicago. Because he was in the area, he stopped in Amherst, Massachusetts, where I was attending college, and took my dormitory floor out to dinner. Without my knowledge, he apparently learned and remembered a great deal about my friends. A week later, my roommate—who was a Hotel/Restaurant/Travel major wanting to become a restaurateur—burst in our room yelling, "Z-Man, your dad sent me a huge package!" Dad had sent a shipment of Kraft cookbooks and restaurant-related literature to Doug. A few minutes later, Cathy down the hall came in laughing. Apparently, she had told my dad that she lived on Kraft Macaroni and Cheese and he had sent her 1,728 (twelve-gross) boxes. Oddly, I half-suspected that Dad thought we were all a bunch of losers who might not amount to anything, but publicly, anyways, he always *assumed the best* about us, *communicating that he cared* and *expecting us to pursue our passions*.

As I began my career as a first grade teacher, Dad continued to be an *excellent resource* for me as well as my young students. He constantly sent educational materials that Kraft produced—usually pertaining to health and nutrition—to any school at which I taught. He sent all my students Kraft Marshmallow book bags for Christmas one year. Another year, an eighteen-wheeler pulled up at our school. My dad had sent thousands of boxes of felt-tip markers that were packaged in Mac 'n Cheese-looking-boxes to be distributed to every student and teacher in the school. He was always *going the extra mile* to *make someone's day*.

My father respected and valued others who worked as hard as he did; as a result, I often consider how much he would have loved so many of you. Thanks for giving so many gifts to our kids again this year. By *identifying and building off their strengths and interests; assuming the best about them; communicating that you care; expecting them to pursue their own passions; serving as an excellent resource;* and *going the extra mile to make their day*, you remind me of my father. Though you did not know him, trust me when I say I can pay you no greater compliment. I close with Christmas gift suggestions from Owen Arnold that my dad once shared with me:

> To your enemy, forgiveness.
> To an opponent, tolerance.

To a friend, your heart.
To a customer, service.
To all, charity.
To every child, a good example.
To yourself, respect.

Thanks for indulging me by reading this Christmas reflection on my father. May you all enjoy the happiest holiday season yet. We are making a living again this year at our school simply by showing up; we are making a life by giving of ourselves so freely while we are here. Thanks for making a difference and a life at our school by *Teaching with Passion* each day!

God Bless Us Everyone!

Jeff

19

Stretching the Culture for Powerful Learning

Creating a Stretch Culture

The following *Friday Focus* was written for the first Friday of the new calendar year at a school where I was serving my first year as principal. At the time of this writing, we had concluded nearly half of the school year. In many ways it was a successful first half of the school year: teachers seemed relatively happy, I had received very few parent complaints, students were performing well in terms of grades and behavior, and I had observed first hand many teachers and students engaged in high-quality learning activities as I visited classrooms each day. At the same time, it seemed to me that we could be doing so much more. Our students came from supportive families and we had very little in the way of what some in education might think of as "challenging" student demographics. Although all available data indicated we were a very *good* school, I could not honestly find a wealth of specific data to indicate that we were a *great* school, one that was recognized throughout the region and state as a school leading the way in student and teacher learning. Although I had spent the first half of the year mostly observing the current school culture and its impact on student learning, I knew that—if we really wanted to effect important school improvement—we would need to make some significant changes relating to our culture and, as principal, I would need to start setting the stage for "stretching" the school's performance by creating a stretch culture.

Robert Eaker has written and spoken extensively about developing what he calls a "stretch" culture. Eaker (2009) focuses on seven things educators can do to create such a culture:

1. Move from "fixed" time to "flexible" time within the school day.

2. Move from "average" learning to "individual" learning.

3. Move from "group" support to "individual" support.

4. Move from "blame and punishment" to "encourage and caring."

5. Move from "teacher tell/student listen" to "teacher coaching/ student practice."

6. Move from "good" to "great."

7. Move from recognizing and celebrating a "few" to creating "lots of winners and celebrating their successes."

To create such a culture—one in which we are constantly pushing ourselves and our students to stretch their learning performance—we must begin by examining the school's mission, first making sure that we have a mission in place that is focused on high levels of learning for all and then aligning our policies, procedures, and practices throughout the school in a way that ensures we are optimizing our ability to make the mission a reality. It is critical to note that "stretching" our school does not mean asking our teachers—or our students—to merely work harder. Instead, we must ensure that everyone in the school is working smarter and in a way that is focused like a laser beam on powerful student learning.

The Nineteenth Friday

For the very first *Friday Focus* writing of the new calendar year, I wanted to set the stage for tweaking our school culture in a way that coincided with guaranteeing high levels of learning for all students and ensuring that the adults in the building were in agreement about what it was we wanted all students to learn in every subject at every grade level. In this school, we did not have a school mission statement or any statements of vision, values, or beliefs. We did have a districtwide mission statement, which we had adopted as our school's mission statement as well, but I wanted to lead the staff through a process of examining this statement and creating statements of vision and values. To begin this process, I spoke at some length about such statements at a faculty meeting earlier in the week. Then, I followed up on my remarks at this staff meeting with the *Friday Focus* memo below, reminding teachers of the importance of a school's mission and how it shapes a school's culture. According to Barth (2002, p. 6), a school's culture is just about the most important aspect of the school, having "…more influence on life and learning in the schoolhouse than the president of the country, the state department of education, the superintendent, the school board, or even the principals, teachers, and parents…." This *Friday Focus* begins by going into further detail about the characteristics of a positive school culture and then focusing on one of these characteristics: a clear purpose, or mission. Next, I discuss how our mission must be centered on student learning and offer several characteristics of powerful learning statements. I knew that as the second half of the school year progressed I would be talking with teachers about our mission, our vision, and our values, and how these could and should drive the work we would do to make certain our school was achieving at the highest levels possible, striving for "great" rather than settling for "good." To get the ball rolling, I asked teachers to informally rank where we currently were on each of the eight characteristics of school culture and start discussing with their colleagues how and why they ranked each characteristic as they did.

Friday Focus!

Friday, January 9

Ultimately, a school's culture has far more influence on life and learning in the schoolhouse than the state department of education, the superintendent, the school board, or even the principal can ever have

— Roland Barth (2002).

A school's culture can indeed be a powerful thing. It can include many components and be defined in many ways. Barth's simplest definition of school culture is, "The way we do things around here." In schools with positive cultures, these "things" are primarily focused on student learning. A culture that consistently focuses on student learning must possess the following characteristics: (a) a clear purpose; (b) a collaborative environment; (c) frequent discussions centered on best teaching practices; (d) a commitment to continuous improvement; (e) a results orientation; (f) administrators who empower teachers; (g) a willingness to confront and overcome adversity; and (h) a staff that always has the best interests of students at heart (Barth, 2002). Everything begins with a clear purpose—or *mission*. As I mentioned at our meeting this week, an organization's mission answers the question why it exists—what, precisely, is its fundamental core purpose? Of course, at any school, it is the educators' *responsibility* to ensure that each of their students is learning at high levels, but at Edgewood, our culture helps us to go beyond mere responsibility. Guaranteeing superior learning for all students is our *passion*.

Many of our students may have received gifts over the recent holiday season, yet none can be as valuable as the gifts their teachers give them throughout the year and which last a lifetime—most importantly, the gift of lifelong learning. Ron Brandt (1998) wrote a book called *Powerful Learning* in which he summarized the learning process to include ten crucial statements. These ten essential fundamentals of learning apply to individual students as well as entire organizations and serve as reminders of how students learn and how we can optimize their ability to achieve at their highest possible levels. Thank you for keeping these statements in mind as we begin another calendar year together of teaching and learning and as we move closer to second semester here at Edgewood:

- People learn what is personally meaningful to them;
- People learn when they accept challenging, but achievable, goals;
- Learning is developmental;
- Individuals learn differently;
- People construct new knowledge by building their current knowledge;
- Much learning occurs through social interaction;
- People need feedback in order to learn;
- Successful learning involves the use of strategies—which themselves must be learned;
- A positive emotional climate strengthens learning;
- Learning is influenced by total environment.

As I continue to observe in classrooms throughout our school each day, I notice our kids learning at high levels because these ten crucial statements are being considered as lessons are planned, implemented, and assessed.

After reading this week's *Friday Focus*, I hope you will take a bit of time to do two things. First, go back to Barth's eight characteristics of a positive school culture. Rank Edgewood on a scale of 1 to 10 for where we are right now. Hopefully, you will find yourself giving our school high marks in many of these areas. Next, take a moment to reflect on where you are individually on a scale of 1 to 10 for each of Brandt's ten characteristics of powerful learning. Again, I hope you find yourself awarding high marks. Although the latter activity is an individual and private one, the former is worth sharing. It might be helpful to share our self-assessments of Edgewood's school culture as we begin to craft vision and value statements to support our current district mission and current School Improvement Plan goals.

At our staff meeting this week, I defined exactly what we mean when we talk about a school's—or any organization's—*mission, vision, and values*. Although these statements must be written with input from the entire school, I did mention one nonnegotiable for a school: the word *learning* must be included when crafting a mission or brief statement of purpose. The more we remember Brandt's advice about powerful learning, the more likely it is that all Edgewood students will learn at high levels. Similarly, the more successful we are at realizing Barth's characteristics of a positive school culture, the more our students will learn.

Thanks for giving the most powerful gift of all each day again this year to our students—the gift of learning. Incorporating these powerful learning practices into our daily lessons and working together to build a positive school culture are two ways that we *Teach with Passion* each day and ensure that we fulfill our mission.

Happy Weekend!

Jeff

20

Creating a Vision

Mission or Vision?

In recent years, almost all schools have worked to create a mission statement of some sort. Of course, some mission statements are more powerful than others, both in terms of the words contained within the mission statement itself and in the way in which the mission statement is publicized, emphasized, monitored, and followed. In addition to a statement of mission, many schools have also crafted vision statements. Although somewhat less prevalent than mission statements, a powerful vision statement is every bit as important as the mission. Although these two statements have become increasingly prevalent at schools in recent years, many educators still confuse the two and often end up writing what I would consider a mission statement as their vision or vice versa.

In essence, a school's mission is its statement of purpose and answers the "Why?" questions: *Why* are we here? *Why* do we serve as educators? As mentioned in the previous chapter, school mission statements can vary from school to school to some extent, but hopefully all would mention the word *learning* as a critical component of the mission. Although the mission answers a "why" question, the vision statement tends to answer a "what" question as in: *What* is it we hope to become? *What* contribution do we want to make to our students and community? Because it can be easy to confuse the two statements, it is important that school leaders spend a certain amount of time educating all staff in the school as to the exact intent of a mission, a vision, and the differences between the two.

The Twentieth Friday

In the *Friday Focus* that follows, I write at length about what a vision statement is and what kinds of questions we would want to start asking when beginning to craft such a statement for our school. As with the mission statement, it is important that we spend just enough time on this to get it right. Although no one wants to devote months or even weeks to creating such statements, spending a bit of time on the front end can save time later in that we will have created strong, practical, and sustainable documents that all staff members understand and recognize as driving forces of the school's culture. Typically, schools might want to begin this process—or revisit current statements—at the beginning of the school year. Because I was a new principal at a school that was performing quite well in many areas, I decided to wait until the new calendar year to begin broaching the topics of mission, vision, and values. In the previous *Friday Focus*, I wrote at length about mission statements, including our school district's current mission. Now it was time to examine the idea of vision statements and begin creating one for our school community.

One can argue that to be great an organization must have a compelling vision statement that is clear and forward focused. Blanchard and Stoner (2004) go as far as stating that all world-class organizations they know are driven by a clear vision and direction that are championed by top leaders in the organization. A clear and compelling vision can help guide the choices that all adults in the school make because they are making such decisions and choices with an end result in mind. An effective vision statement is a starting point for future greatness: "It starts everything in the right direction and—if followed up by effective implementation, positive consequence, and sustainability strategies—will keep things going in the right direction. Vision is the difference between business as usual and a world-class organization" (Blanchard & Stoner, 2004, p. 28). Although I am in complete agreement regarding the profound importance of vision within any organization, I am also aware that their words include a rather prodigious "if." A vision is only powerful *if* we implement it effectively, recognize and celebrate those who are working to achieve the it, and devise strategies for ensuring the vision stands as a sustainable force. In schools with positive, productive cultures, teachers and administrators work together to ensure that this important *if* is resolved.

Friday Focus!

Friday, January 16

There is no more powerful engine driving an organization toward excellence and long-range success than an attractive, worthwhile, and achievable vision of the future, widely shared.

— Burt Nanus (1992, p. 3).

Just this week, we celebrated Martin Luther King Jr. by observing our annual national holiday in his honor. Like many of you, perhaps, I still admire this man and so much of what he stood for. Two years ago, our family even drove to Memphis, Tennessee, to see the former Lorraine Hotel, site of MLK's assassination—which is now part of an impressive civil rights museum—because I wanted my daughter to learn more about this good and decent man. Although it is easy at times to forget the actual reason for many holidays, I do try to keep this man's noble work in mind throughout the year. One might ask how this personal aside relates to our school. Well, recently, I have been talking about our need to examine our school/district mission and to create a vision for ourselves as a school community. When considering the idea of a *vision*, what better place to start than MLK's "I have a dream…" speech. His vision—expressed in this brief, but powerful speech—is a lasting and dramatic example of the power that can be generated by creating and communicating a compelling vision of the future.

As I mentioned in a faculty meeting recently, a school's vision addresses the "what" question: "What kind of school do we hope to become?" or "If we are true to our purpose now, what might we become at some point in the future?" If we do not decide what an ideal Edgewood Middle School looks like, we will not be able to adopt programs, enact ideas, create policies, or behave in ways that move us to this ideal state. Getting from point A to point B requires knowing exactly where point B is and recognizing what it will take to get there and what it will look like when we arrive. Vision instills an organization with a sense of direction. It articulates a vivid picture of the future so compelling that its members will be motivated to work together to make it a reality. Like a Specific, Measurable, Attainable, Results Oriented, and Time Bound (SMART) goal, our vision should be credible, focused on the essential, and used as a blueprint for improvement.

Here are a few random vision statements I admire from organizations other than K–12 education, which seem to fulfill the description listed above:

1. From The Sea Island Company on Sea Island, Georgia: "To be known as the finest resort and resort community in the world as recognized by our employees, members, guests, and the industry."

2. From a John F. Kennedy speech: "By the end of the decade, we will put a man on the moon."

3. From McDonald's: "McDonald's vision is to be the world's best quick service restaurant experience. Being the best means providing outstanding quality, service, cleanliness, and value, so that we make every customer in every restaurant smile."

4. From McCaw Cellular Communications: "To develop a reliable wireless network that empowers people with the freedom to travel anywhere—across the hall or across the continent—and communicate effortlessly."

5. From the University of Kansas (Wichita) School of Medicine: "We will be the premier center for community-oriented medical education, scholarship, patient care, service, and research. Our leadership will revolutionize the delivery of health care in Kansas and beyond."

Wow! Vision statements can indeed be powerful and motivating proclamations of organizational direction and focus. At the school level, a faculty that works together to craft a clear, shared vision of the school they are attempting to create benefits in a number of ways:

1. Shared vision motivates and energizes people;
2. Shared vision creates a proactive orientation;
3. Shared vision gives direction to people within the organization;
4. Shared vision establishes specific standards of excellence;
5. Shared vision creates a clear agenda for action (DuFour & Eaker, 1998).

I look forward to working with all staff members in the near future to co-create a bold and compelling vision statement for our school that should stand for the next three to five years, at which time, it would need revisiting to gauge our progress. As we work together in this process, it is helpful to consider several questions to guide the vision development process:

1. What would you like to see our school become?
2. What reputation would it have?
3. What contribution would it make to our students and our community?
4. How would people work together?
5. What values would it embody?
6. When I leave this school, I would like to be remembered for....
7. I want my school to be a place where....
8. The kind of school I would like my own child to attend would....
9. The kind of school I would like to teach in would....
10. What could we accomplish in the next five years that would make us proud?

A vision will have little impact unless it is widely shared and accepted and connects with the personal visions of those within the school. Building a common vision for the future can be a difficult process and can even be—at times—a contentious process. As we embark upon this, we must help each other identify common causes, interests, goals, and aspirations. Every school in the world is a unique learning community requiring a unique vision statement. At Edgewood, we are blessed with amazing students, awesome teachers, and fabulous parent and community support. As a result, creating a vision for our school should be an exciting venture. Thanks for joining me in this process beginning at our next staff meeting!

Having a clear and agreed upon vision for what we want to become and achieve is a vital way that we *Teach with Passion* each day.

Happy Weekend!

Jeff

21

Homework Perspectives

Trends in Homework Philosophies

Like many aspects of education, it seems as if we have seen a cyclical trend in homework practices and philosophies in our schools. The discourse regarding homework is one that excites the passions not only of educators, but also parents, who are, of course, the people most likely to observe the extent to which their children are engaged in—and successfully completing—high-quality (and, alas, low-quality) homework assignments. In researching homework trends in our public schools during recent history, one may conclude that the amount of homework assigned in schools rises and falls with concomitant events occurring in the larger world around us. Data shows that the amount of homework high school students completed in the 1950s and 1960s increased from previous decades, perhaps in response to broader issues associated with the Cold War. In the late 1960s and 1970s, interest in homework as a major issue in education waned. This period of de-emphasizing homework proved temporary, however, as a renewed concern about declining education standards culminated in the 1983 report *A Nation at Risk* which again suggested we were falling behind other nations in terms of academic excellence and called on educators—among other things—to assign far more homework for high school students (National Commission on Excellence in Education, 1983). During his tenure as our nation's Secretary of Education, William Bennett also endorsed the virtues of homework and provided specific guidelines for educators to consider regarding homework (U.S. Department of Education, 1986). This push for more homework as a way to raise student achievement enjoyed the support of educators, parents, and policymakers throughout the 1980s and 1990s.

In recent years, however, it seems as if the tide may once again be shifting against the practice of homework. With an increasing number of children living in single parent homes or homes in which both parents are working long hours, the support for homework may be waning. In addition to the hectic lives of parents, our kids' lives seem to be increasingly filled with structured activities around the clock, making time for homework completion increasingly difficult to find. Although most parents still support the idea of homework—only 10% of parents believed their children had too much homework in a nationwide poll conducted in 2000 (Public Agenda, 2000)—most principals and teachers with whom I have worked in recent years have fielded a significant number of calls from parents on the opposite side of the spectrum, who state that there are simply not enough hours in the day to participate in after school activities, enjoy a family mealtime, and still complete more than an hour of homework on a given night.

Homework remains a hot-button issue in the education profession and is one for which there is no simple answer pleasing to all stakeholders. Yet, it is vitally important that the professionals directly involved—teachers and administrators—examine this issue thoroughly and come to agreement regarding the purpose of homework and how best we achieve this purpose by employing best practices.

The Twenty-First Friday

The following *Friday Focus* starts off by juxtaposing two diametrically opposing points of view relating to homework in our public schools, one from Robert Marzano and the other from Alfie Kohn. Anyone who has served as an educator for any length of time is likely familiar with these two viewpoints. My point in sharing the two quotes as a starting point for this *Friday Focus* was to suggest that both have their merits, but that we needed to focus our attention on what our true purpose is in assigning homework before deciding what our practices should be. In schools with thriving school cultures focused on learning, the issue of homework is not left to chance and individual choice. Instead, the issue is discussed openly, with all voices heard, but ending with consensus as to what our practices will be as professional educators. At the time of this writing, I was still only halfway into my first year as principal at this school, but it was already clear that our school's homework policies and practices were all over the map, both across grade levels and subject areas. On more than one occasion, parents had called to voice concerns about homework practices being employed in many classrooms at our school which were, in all candor, difficult to defend. Although I always worked to support our school's outstanding teachers, I also realized that we needed to initiate a dialogue on this important issue which mattered deeply to our teachers, our students, and our parents. What follows is the first of a two-part *Friday Focus* on the issue of homework. In it, I begin the discussion by sharing some research regarding the positive and negative effects of homework, as well as the three general types of homework we assign and the purposes of each.

Friday Focus!

Friday, January 23

Homework and practice are ways of extending the school day and providing students with opportunities to refine and extend their knowledge. Teachers can use both of these practices as powerful instructional tools.

— Marzano, Pickering, & Pollock (2001, p. 71)

No research has ever demonstrated any academic benefit to making kids do homework before they're in high school. Even in high school, there is only a weak correlation between standard measures of achievement and doing homework. What's more, there is no evidence that the two are causally related—that is, that kids who have better grades and test scores have them because they've had to do more academic assignments after a full day in school. Finally, there isn't a shred of evidence to demonstrate that homework has any nonacademic advantages, such as teaching self-discipline and responsibility or teaching kids good work habits.

— Alfie Kohn (2006)

Well, these are two decidedly opposing points of view regarding the wisdom of assigning homework in schools. Honestly, I find myself somewhere in between Marzano and Kohn, both of whom enjoy wide respect as educational researchers, writers, and thinkers. On the one hand, I believe that carefully thought out and clearly communicated homework assignments can improve student learning. On the other hand, I have seen students on both ends of the achievement spectrum become frustrated by homework: Our overachievers spend too much time agonizing over homework to the detriment of family and extracurricular activities; our struggling students, meanwhile, may not even complete the homework.

Secretly, I was never much of a homework assigner as a teacher—at the elementary, middle, or even high school level. However, I do agree with the by-now-well-known rule of thumb suggesting that we should follow the ten-minute per grade-level amount. For those of us at Edgewood, then, our sixth graders should have no more than sixty minutes of homework each night whereas our eighth graders should have no more than eighty minutes nightly. Probably the foremost expert researcher on homework is Harris Cooper from Duke University who finds that such amounts of homework promote student learning at the middle and high school levels. However, he also finds a negative effect for any additional amounts, suggesting that between seven and twelve total hours of homework a week should be the maximum, even at the high school level.

I raise this issue partly out of my own personal reservations about huge amounts of homework (I have a ninth grade daughter who will—if given the choice—forego food, sleep, and family in order to complete all assigned homework) and partly because I have heard from several parents this year who expressed similar concerns. At the middle school level, especially, I believe it is important to stick to the sixty-, seventy-, eighty-minute maximum at each grade level. In addition, we must find ways to communicate with each other to ensure that we are working collaboratively in assigning homework. If I have students working one hour on my subject tonight, my teammates cannot also assign an hour of homework each.

One could write volumes on this topic, but space limits me to just a few words. Let me expend several by sharing Cooper's (2006) pros and cons of homework and Marzano's (2007) three purposes for homework, as well as how to communicate these assignments with parents.

Cooper describes several positive effects of homework:

- Immediate achievement and learning, including better retention, understanding, and critical thinking;

- Long-term academic effects, including better study habits and attitude toward school;

- Nonacademic effects, including better self-direction, self-discipline, time management, and independent problem solving; and,

- Greater parental appreciation of and involvement in schooling.

As well as some negative effects:

- Satiation, including loss of interest in subject and physical and mental fatigue;

- Denial of access to leisure-time and community activities;

- Parental interference, including pressure and confusion of instructional techniques;

- Cheating; and,

- Increased differences between high and low achievers.

Marzano recommends three general types of homework: (a) homework that helps students *deepen their knowledge* (e.g., compare two political systems we have been studying); (b) homework that *enhances students' fluency* with procedural knowledge (e.g., solve multiplication problems quickly, checking for speed and accuracy); and (c) homework that *introduces new content* (e.g., read a section of a book that the teacher has not addressed but will address the following day). For each piece of homework assigned, Marzano (2007) insists that teachers should *communicate with parents regarding the assignment* and even offers *sample scripts:*

> The homework tonight is to introduce your child to poetry terms before we study them tomorrow in class. The assignment is to read pages 56–62 in the textbook. Remind your child that the content in those pages will be reviewed tomorrow. However, also remind them that it is important to complete the assignment so that he/she has some basic understanding of poetry terms. You can help by asking your child to summarize what he or she has learned as a result of reading those pages. You can also ask your child to write out at least two questions he or she has about what was read.

The issue of homework provokes wide ranges of opinions from Alfie Kohn, who would pretty much be willing to eliminate it completely, to researchers who would assign even more than the ten-minute-per-grade-level guideline advocated by Marzano and others. I continue to argue for small, meaningful amounts of homework that provide opportunities for practice or fluency and to prime the pump for future learning. Whatever your own personal views might be, thanks for adhering to the time guidelines cited herein and for communicating with teammates so we do not overwhelm our kids with too much on any given night. Finally, thanks for communicating with parents about what their child's homework assignments are and what role the parents can play in assisting. Planning for meaningful homework, working with teammates to coordinate homework assignments, and communicating with parents regarding their child's homework assignments are a few more ways we *Teach with Passion* each day at our school!

Have an Awesome Weekend

Jeff

22

Homework Practices

A Homework Fable

Steven Wright, principal of Good Middle School (GMS) in Anyplace, USA, was finishing up some last-minute tasks in his office on a warm summer day. Teachers and students at GMS would be returning to school in a few short weeks and there was much to be completed still, yet he was confident that another successful year of teaching and learning lurked just around the corner. Suddenly, the school secretary interrupted his planning to let him know that a family wanted to see him. The family was relocating to the area and considering enrolling their seventh grade daughter at Good Middle, but wanted to meet the principal first. This was always one of Dr. Wright's favorite summertime tasks; he enjoyed showing prospective students and their parents around the school and bragging about its many fine programs, teachers, and facilities. He immediately dropped what he was doing to meet the family and welcome them to the area.

Dr. Wright introduced himself to the parents, Mr. and Mrs. Watson, and their daughter, Sally. He invited them on a tour of the campus, showing them several classrooms, each equipped with state-of-the-art resources, including interactive whiteboards, document cameras, and several computers. He walked them by the new gymnasium, as well as by the school's auditorium, cafeteria, and media center. After touring the facility, Wright invited the Watson family into his office to discuss the school's academic offerings, extracurricular activities, and the highly qualified teaching staff. The Watsons seemed most impressed with everything they had seen and all that they had heard from Dr. Wright. As they were getting up to leave, Mr. Watson indicated that they would likely be enrolling Sally at Good Middle the following week. Mrs. Watson interrupted to mention that she had one final question for Dr. Wright. She asked, "Will Sally have regular homework in all her classes and, if so, what types of homework assignments should she anticipate?" Dr. Wright hesitated, fidgeting uncomfortably. For a fleeting moment, he considered a completely truthful answer, but that would have sounded something along the lines of: "To be honest, folks, I can't really say. As a matter of fact, when it comes to homework, you'll basically be playing the educational lottery game here at Good Middle. Depending on a roll of the dice, your daughter will have teachers who may or may not assign lots of homework. Furthermore, the chances that she will be assigned quality homework assignments for practice or preparation, as opposed to mindless busy work, are also completely random. You see, we leave this up to the individual teachers, all of whom—as professional educators—have differing thoughts on the important issue of homework." Rather than proceed with this version, Dr. Wright mumbled something to the effect that teachers tried to communicate with each other to make sure that students did complete regular homework assignments and that these homework assignments were scheduled so that no student would have more than an hour or two of homework on any given night, but that the exact amount of homework Sally would have depended to some extent on which teachers she had. The Watsons seemed a bit leery of Wright's vague answer, but thanked him again for his time and departed the building.

The Twenty-Second Friday

The fictional scenario above may well contain more truth than fiction for many principals. Even in schools that have spent a great deal of time working to align the curriculum, create common assessments, and collectively analyze data, the issue of aligning homework practices has been neglected or completely ignored. It is evident from the previous *Friday Focus*, as well as the one that follows, that our own school still had work to do in the area of planning for, communicating about, and implementing best practices relating to homework. Although we had homework "policies" at all grade levels, each year problems still arose, resulting in some parents insisting there was way too much homework, while others were convinced there was not nearly enough. Even more important to us, as educators, was the type of homework that was being assigned and for what purposes. In the previous *Friday Focus*, I concentrated primarily on different homework philosophies. In the following memo, I focus more on homework practices. I suggest that all teachers keep in mind "PRP" as a mnemonic device to represent the legitimate reasons we should assign homework for practice, review, and preparation. I also offer a few specific practices teachers can implement to increase the chances that all students complete all assignments.

Friday Focus!

Friday, January 31

Simply assigning homework may not produce the desired effect—in fact, ill-structured homework might even have a negative effect on stu-

dent achievement. Teachers must carefully plan and assign homework in a way that maximizes the potential for student success.

— Marzano (2007, p. 77)

Last week, I penned and shared part one of a two-part FF on the always-challenging issue of homework. Even after twenty-eight years in teaching, I continue to have more questions than answers relating to homework, but it is something we, as a team of professional educators, should consider collectively—and continuously.

To review just a bit from my previous FF on homework, one issue to consider is the *purpose* of homework. It may be helpful to think of assigning homework for *PRP*: *Practice* (the material has already been taught and is being emphasized for fluency), *Review* (bringing all the facts, details, vocabulary together; applying what they have learned), and *Prepare* for future learning (careful, though, on this one; although OK to assign homework that asks students to begin thinking about a topic they will be studying, it can be counterproductive to have them read ahead to learn material that has yet to be taught). Another issue to consider is *time*. I mentioned previously the well-known guideline of ten minutes per grade level, but at times, we might assign something that we think will take only twenty minutes when, in reality, it may take students much longer (we, as teachers, possess the "curse of knowledge"; i.e., we sometimes think something is easy, quick, or obvious to all because it is second nature to us as experts in our subject area). A good idea is to check in periodically with students to see if the time they are spending on homework assignments is commensurate with your expectations. You might even create a homework assignment calendar similar to one suggested by Marzano, Pickering, and Pollock (2001, p. 65) but including a time component:

Subject: _____

Due Date: _____

What I Have to Do Tonight: _____

Purpose of Assignment: _____

What I Have to Already Know or be Able to Do in Order to Complete the Assignment: _____

Anticipated/Actual Time Needed to Complete: _____ / _____

A final issue to consider is how best to get our students to actually complete all homework assignments. This has been a challenge for every teacher at some point in his or her career, if not every year. Although frustrating, one thing that will *not* work is punitive measures. The threat of low grades or zeroes only motivates students who are motivated by grades to begin with. This would, therefore, work effectively with our valedictorian, but our valedictorian is unlikely to be blowing off many homework assignments in the first place. Alas, there is no easy answer for those students most at risk of not turning in homework, but here are a few ideas I found in researching this topic—these come mainly from Jane Bluestein (2008), Linda Darling-Hammond and Olivia Ifill-Lynch (2006), and just a bit of yours truly:

- *Assign work that is worthy of the effort:* Does it make sense? Is it necessary? Is it useful? Is it authentic and engaging?

- *Make the work doable:* Be sure directions are clear and that students can complete the assignment without help.

- *Match assignments to student needs:* Reach out to students who are not completing homework and brainstorm strategies that work for them. Assign independent work at or near their proficiency level.

- *Create space and time for completing "home" work at school:* Complete at school: before/after lunch, etc. As schools, we must continue to find systematic strategies for dealing with missing assignments.

- *Make work public:* Display exemplars of proficient student work so they know what is expected. Talk students through the evening's requirements.

- *Encourage collaboration:* Among students (eighth graders helping sixth graders or classmates occasionally working together on an assignment) and among staff (communicating about amounts assignments and supporting each other by sharing ideas and assignments with the highest return rate).

- *Offer students choices:* Find ways, when appropriate, for students to choose how they will extend learning, based on their interest or talent.

- *Build flexibility into your homework policy:* At the outset, plan for the likelihood of some students not completing work and find ways for students to recover, while still holding them accountable for completing the work.

- *Communicate with parents:* Parents need to understand the purposes of homework, the amount of homework that will be assigned, consequences for not completing homework, and a description of the types of parental involvement that are appropriate. Make this explicit up front and reinforce periodically.

- *Always provide feedback of some sort, but vary your feedback practices to make this viable:* Although it is probably not feasible to formally assess every piece of student homework, the more feedback we can provide, the more likely we raise completion rates. Employ strategies that help manage the workload, collaborating with colleagues on best ways to accomplish this.

A survey conducted by Public Agenda (2000), a nonprofit, nonpartisan research group, found that 50% of parents surveyed said they have had a serious argument with their children over homework and 34% said it became a source of struggle and stress for them and their children. By following some or all of the above bullet points (perhaps none more important than communicating at the outset with parents about your expectations and letting them know how they can—and cannot—help their children with homework), we can reduce this level of strife while increasing our students' homework completion rate.

As a final note, although I have written two FFs on the topic of homework, it is important to mention to everyone that—overall—I believe Edgewood teachers do an outstanding job in this regard. It is also important, however, to revisit our homework practices regularly to ensure that they are producing results which are helping our students learn, grow, and succeed. Thanks for planning and assigning homework that maximizes chances for student success; it is yet another way we *Teach with Passion* each day at our school!

Have an Awesome Weekend

Jeff

23

Tips for Teaching Reading, Part I

Reading Strategies in the Content Areas

It is increasingly clear that the teaching of reading is important—and difficult. Moreover, it is becoming increasingly obvious that we need to devote more attention to the teaching of reading not only at the early elementary levels, but also at the middle and high school levels. To close learning gaps that exist in the middle and high school grades, teachers need to understand the complex process of learning how to read and to realize that to succeed in any content area—from chemistry, to history, to math—students must succeed as readers.

Unfortunately, many teachers, both young and veteran alike, have had little in the way of formal training in teaching reading, particularly if they teach at the middle school or high school levels. Therefore, it is critically important that schools provide training on how to teach reading effectively across all content areas and all grade levels. To teach all children to read, six areas must be addressed, according to Denton (2000):

- *Early assessment* to identify each child's individual needs and detect problems early;

- *Classroom reading instruction* that meets the needs of all children;

- *Early intervention* to help children who are at risk of not learning;

- *Intervention for older children* who are not reading at grade level;

- *Teacher education* that prepares new teachers to meet every child's reading needs; and

- *Professional development* that helps teachers continually improve their skills in teaching reading (p. 1).

Denton emphasizes that central to each of the above areas are the last two: teacher education and professional development. In recent years, with the advent of Adequate Yearly Progress (AYP) accountability, many schools across the nation have established school improvement plans with increased reading proficiency as a vital component of the plan for improvement. Unfortunately, in most schools—particularly at the secondary level—very few teachers in the building possess a wealth of expertise in teaching reading, making progress toward schoolwide goals a crapshoot at best unless school leaders dedicate professional development time to training all teachers in all content areas how to teach reading.

Although helping teachers of all grade levels and content areas to teach their students how to become better readers may seem daunting at first, it does not have to be so, particularly if we focus on keeping it simple and remembering that less is more. Implementing a professional development session in which all teachers in attendance learn one or two practical techniques for effectively teaching reading is ultimately more beneficial to the entire student population than if 3 or 4 teachers walk away with a zillion of ideas and tons of enthusiasm. A simple way to help all teachers in the school to become better teachers of reading is to remind them of three basic steps we can consciously take into account when we are tackling any reading assignment:

- *Step 1:* Before Reading Strategies (brainstorming, skimming, predicting, activating prior knowledge, learning crucial vocabulary);

- *Step 2:* During Reading Strategies (rereading, inferring, questioning, thinking aloud, summarizing); and,

- *Step 3:* After Reading Strategies (rereading, confirming predictions, clarifying, reflecting, analyzing, synthesizing).

If we can get all teachers in all subject areas to focus on some or all of these before, during, and after reading strategies when assigning a content area reading, we can take a giant first step toward improving reading achievement throughout the school.

The Twenty-Third Friday

The following *Friday Focus* represents the third instance in this book (see also the *Friday Focus* writings on Differentiated Instruction [page 26] and Homework [page 88]) that stands as one in a two-part *Friday Focus* series. This *Friday Focus* and the one that follows in Chapter 25 relate to the topic of teaching reading in all content areas, not just English and Language Arts classes. In this *Friday Focus* writing, I begin our discussion by writing about something which may seem elementary, but which I have seen used effectively in grades K–12: *learning walls*. At the elementary level, one is more likely to see these referred to as "word walls," and I have seen them called by other names as well, but whatever we call them, posting academic content words, phrases, and concepts within each classroom can have a powerful impact on student learning and can help both struggling and proficient students alike incorporate content area vocabulary into their own learning.

Each content area has its own language or vocabulary. This vocabulary can be rather generic or highly technical and we must provide systematic and specific strategies for ensuring that our students master this content-specific language. Because vocabulary knowledge and reading comprehension are so directly related, it will help students become more proficient in the content area and also more proficient as readers. Teachers must provide direct instruction to students relating to vocabulary acquisition, modeling how to use context clues to determine meanings of new words, and providing students with multiple exposures to new vocabulary across contexts in order to ensure a deeper understanding of the words' meanings. In this *Friday Focus* and the one in the next chapter, I draw on the expertise of Dr. Sharon Faber who has written and spoken extensively on the topic of teaching reading—even if you're not a reading teacher.

Friday Focus!

Friday, February 7

Reading is the most important subject in school. It's more important than all the other subjects combined. If a child can't learn to read well and love to read, the chances of that kid finding success and happiness on any level are low....[S]uccessful kids represent the spectrum of all racial, religious, economic, and cultural diversity possible, but they all have one thing in common: they read well and love it....I want my students to understand that their ability to read and write is a matter of life and death....[S]how me a good reader and I'll show you a child with strong self esteem....[L]ives hang in the balance. If you do nothing else as a teacher, develop able and passionate readers.

— Rafe Esquith (2003)

Wow—reading really is quite important! I first heard Rafe Esquith speak during a NPR interview several years ago. His comments about teaching—and teaching reading, specifically—were so compelling that I listened intently to the entire interview and proceeded to immediately purchase two of his books, *There are No Shortcuts* (2003) and *Teach Like Your Hair's on Fire: The Methods and Madness Inside Room 56* (2007). Ultimately, I have mixed thoughts on his books, but I still recall the interview as being profoundly moving. He touched on many subjects, and I wanted to reiterate his message regarding the lifelong importance of reading and how it is imperative that we all serve as reading teachers, regardless of our primary content area.

Writing about how to teach reading would fill several hundred *Friday Focus* memos of space—at a minimum. However, I would like to share just one resource and one strategy from that resource. The resource is a great book, *How to Teach Reading When You're Not a Reading Teacher* (2006) by my friend Dr. Sharon Faber. Sharon's extremely readable book contains many ideas, but I want to highlight just one: *Learning Walls*—not an original idea of Sharon's by any means, and seemingly an elementary one at that, but one she has written about extensively and specifically in her book as a way to connect kids to academic vocabulary.

Learning walls can be an effective way for students to associate meaning with the words they will use in each content area. I encourage all teachers at our school to use such walls. First, generate a list of essential words, phrases, concepts, formulas, or whatever students must know depending on the particular content area. Have the learning wall in a prominent place in the classroom where students will be exposed to and can interact with words before, during, and after being introduced to the content. Refer to the wall often, adding pictures, phrases, or color-coding dots as you learn more about each term. You can start by simply writing each term on a 4×6 index card and sticking them on the wall. You may use one color for words sharing a common concept, theme, chapter, or unit of study. Select only those words that students will see and use often in readings related to your class. Remind students on a regular basis that knowing the terms will help them in their reading and writing.

Finally, try to include an activity or comment about words on the learning wall every day. The more students use the words, the more they will retain them. One simple way Faber suggests is to start class by "guessing the word." Choose a word, formula, concept, etc. from the learning wall. Have students number from 1 to 5 on a piece of paper. Give five clues; after each clue, students write their guesses next to the corresponding number. By the fifth clue, everyone should have guessed correctly. The first clue is always the same: "It's one of the words on the learning wall." Add clues as appropriate for numbers two to four. Another idea Sharon suggests is "Wordo," which is similar to Bingo. Make Wordo sheets with the number of empty squares depending on the number of words from the learning wall you want to use. Laminate the sheets so they can be reused. Have students write a different word from the learning wall into each of the blank squares so that every card will be unique. Give students objects to cover the words, having them do so as you call out each word. Like Bingo, the first to cover a row, four corners, or an entire card would win, although you can raise the difficulty level by requiring the winner to define each word as it is called back.

There are six critical elements to using a learning wall successfully (Cunningham, 1999):

- Be selective, including the most essential items needed for mastery of your subject.

- Add words gradually—perhaps five per week.

- Make words accessible by putting the wall where everyone can see it. Use big black letters and colors (according to some research, black ink on yellow paper stimulates learning).

- Practice the words daily by writing, using, chanting.

- Make sure Learning Wall words are spelled correctly in all student work.

- Plan a variety of review activities to provide practice until mastery is achieved.

Esquith equates reading to a life-and-death situation. Although perhaps not literally true, reading well is certainly necessary for success in every walk of life, including every classroom in our school. Teaching reading in all content areas is a key component to our school improvement plan and rightly so. Using learning walls is one way we can teach reading across all content areas. The power of visualization is part of long term memory and a reading strategy we can use to help our students master difficult academic vocabulary. Taking the time to help our students make sense of difficult reading material and academic vocabulary is one way that we *Teach with Passion* each day at our school!

Have an Awesome Weekend

Jeff

24

Tips for Teaching Reading, Part II

The Twenty-Fourth Friday

In the previous chapter, I discussed the importance of making certain that teachers across all grade levels and content areas engage students in explicit and systematic *before*, *during*, and *after* reading strategies when assigning readings. Many of these strategies can apply to more than one of these three steps. One such strategy is a "think aloud," which can be used during all three steps to increase the likelihood that students will comprehend and recall content and vocabulary. A think aloud is a great strategy to slow down the reading process, allowing students a chance to see how skilled readers (i.e., the teacher) interact with and construct meaning from a text. Because most teachers are, themselves, highly successful readers, they take for granted that which struggling readers find quite complex: how to read, understand, and analyze academic writing. Educators must take what they do as readers—without even thinking they are doing it—and break this down for their students, explicitly showing them how they interact with the text and make meaning of unfamiliar content and vocabulary.

Skillful readers unconsciously use a wide range of strategies to make meaning from text they are reading. The think aloud strategy involves modeling these strategies by "thinking aloud" while reading and responding to a text. Strategies for thinking aloud can range from activating prior knowledge, to setting a purpose for reading, to decoding text for meaning, to making personal connections, to making predictions, to visualizing, to asking questions, to monitoring understanding and summarizing, and to applying what has been learned. Using any or all of these strategies, teachers can model think-aloud reading with their students. Teachers can choose to begin the process by explicitly stating what strategies they will be using and why each of these strategies is helpful to the reading process. They may also ask students to take notes on the strategies they are using and why they do so, or to annotate the text by noting words/phrases/passages that triggered the use of a particular strategy. As with most reading strategies, there are a wide variety of ways teachers can implement think-alouds. In the *Friday Focus* that follows, I rely on what Dr. Sharon Faber has written about the strategy of think-alouds. I also share a simple postreading technique Faber calls a "3–2–1 Strategy Chart," which she suggests using as a way to reinforce what has been learned through the reading by summarizing key ideas, rethinking these ideas, and asking questions about what has just been read. In my writing, I also let teachers know that I am placing a hard copy of a 3–2–1 Reading Chart in all their mailboxes. I have found that sometimes teachers read the *Friday Focus* and think they will get around to trying an idea but then forget. Whenever appropriate, I like to increase the likelihood of teachers actually using the ideas by including an attachment or a hard copy handout in mailboxes.

Both the think-aloud and the 3–2–1 strategies are extremely simple ideas that require very little in the way of training or understanding. Nearly any teacher at any school could immediately take either of these two strategies and employ them in their classroom the very next day. Although some content area teachers may initially resist learning about and using reading strategies in their classrooms, I have found that when the ideas are as simple and as practical—not to mention beneficial to students—as the two below, even our most resistant teachers are willing to give it a try.

Friday Focus!

Friday, February 14

Harry Wong says, "The number one problem in the classroom is not discipline, it is the lack of procedures and routines." A similar thing may be said about reading: The number one problem is not students' inability to read, it is their lack of basic reading strategies.

— Sharon Faber (2006, p. 47)

Last week, I referenced Sharon Faber and discussed her ideas regarding learning walls. This week, I wanted to share two additional ideas Sharon discusses frequently and advocates using regularly in all content areas: *Think Alouds* and a *3–2–1 Strategy Chart*. Faber writes at some length about what good readers do *before*, *during*, and *after* reading. As teachers, most of us are strong readers and take these things for granted, not even conscious that we are doing them. Yet many students at the middle school or high school level do not possess these habits at all and must be taught to acquire them. Although prereading and postreading activities are critically important, I wanted to start by focusing on *what good readers do as they read*.

According to Faber (2006), good readers have movies and conversations going in their minds as they read. They read with a purpose and look for information that relates to that purpose. They visualize in their minds what is happening in the text as they read. Good readers build meaning as they read and frequently make predictions about what is to come. They monitor their understanding of the text, making adjustments in their reading as necessary. Good readers try to determine the meaning of unfamiliar words and concepts they come across. Good readers question what is confusing to them in their reading and identify ways to figure out what has confused them.

As good readers ourselves, one of the best ways we can encourage our kids to do any and all of the above while they read is to model this for them through the use of *Think Alouds*. Try it in your class, whether you teach English, math, science, or any other subject. Read aloud from a text or passage of any kind, stopping after awhile and "thinking aloud," demonstrating how to make connections that lead to better comprehension of what is being read. Although you should plan this out, make it seem spontaneous, modeling strategies for solving problems as we read. Simulate such problems, thinking aloud how they can be solved, and showing students what to do when something is hard to understand. Some techniques to model include:

1. Stop and read back to the part you didn't understand or read forward skipping—temporarily—confusing words.

2. Reflect on what you have read and see if there is an inference or explanation you can make.

3. Seek information beyond the text (from a partner or second source) in order to understand.

4. Make a prediction as to what the author/text will state next.

5. Stop to express confusion but indicate you will keep reading to see if the author explains what you don't understand.

Think Alouds can be used easily in any lesson that requires students to read and tend to make a teacher's oral reading exercises more engaging and understandable for all students.

A good and simple strategy for a postreading activity is the *3–2–1 Strategy Chart*. This strategy requires students to summarize key ideas, rethink these ideas in order to focus on information they found interesting or difficult, and then ask one question about what they still want to know. The 3–2–1 chart can be adapted to suit your purpose, but the basic format is for students to write:

- 3 key ideas I found out from the reading
- 2 things that were especially interesting or especially hard to understand
- 1 question I still have

A variation:

- 3 differences between: _____ and: _____
- 2 similarities between them
- 1 question I still have

I will place a copy of a 3–2–1 chart in your box or you can create your own. After students complete their forms, use their responses to construct an outline, complete a graphic organizer, identify sequence, isolate cause and effect, or whatever is logical based on the reading. These responses can also form the basis for a class discussion of the reading, too. Students will be more motivated because the discussion is based on ideas they found and consider important.

No reading strategy will work with all students and some teachers do better with different types of strategies. Regardless of the strategies we use, it is important to understand that if we expect our students to *use* the strategy, we must actually *teach and model* these strategies. Students must internalize the strategies so that these become a part of how they read in all their subject areas. Finding reading strategies is relatively easy; teaching these to students and using them regularly is harder. Yet, doing so—through the use of simple ideas like *Think Alouds* and *3–2–1 Strategy Charts*—is another way we *Teach with Passion* each day at our school!

Have an Awesome Weekend

Jeff

25

A Culture of Curiosity and Passion

The Twenty-Fifth Friday

In Chapter 17, I discussed my practice of periodically using the *Friday Focus* memo to basically write a book review, sharing key information with teachers about a book I read that related in some way(s) to the work we do as educators. The *Friday Focus* below is another example of such a book review memo and—like the version offered in Chapter 17—focuses on a book that is not intended for educators, in this case Thomas Friedman's *The World is Flat: A Brief History of the Twenty-First Century* (2006). Although I read a great deal of professional literature written by and intended for educators, I also enjoy reading current literature that does not relate directly to teaching, but, instead, to private organizations, leadership and management, and current trends in society as a whole. There are several reasons why it is these books that I most often share with teachers. Most importantly, I like to examine such books to see if we can draw parallels between education and that place we hear about so often as teachers: "The real world." Often, I find that a huge overlap exists between the two; the challenges facing business leaders are not unlike the challenges facing educational leaders. The rapid onslaught of technological advances poses both opportunities and challenges to world leaders and school teachers alike. What works in the "real" world often works in schools; what does not work in the "real" world is unlikely to work in schools. Our kids periodically ask us how they will ever use that which they are learning in school once they enter "the real world." It is important that we educators keep abreast of events, advances, and philosophies of the private, government, and civic sectors so that we can answer this question. In doing so, we will realize just how closely we are aligned with all non-educational organizations, what we can learn from each other, and how we can communicate this to our kids so that they will be better prepared for the future that awaits them.

Although Friedman devotes only a small amount of space in his massive book to education, he indirectly answers the "How are we going to use this in the real world?" question by suggesting that the only thing that will matter in this esoteric realm is the ability and desire to keep learning, to be able to access and use information in a rapidly changing environment. In the following *Friday Focus*, I concentrate on two points Friedman makes and relate them to our school. Although the message will be affirming to many teachers, many other teachers need to be reminded that in today's society—both in schools and the "real" world—*how* we learn may well be more important than *what* we are learning.

Friday Focus!

Friday, February 21

Simply providing more *education is probably a good thing on balance, especially if a more educated labor force is a more flexible labor force that can cope more readily with nonroutine tasks and constant occupational change. But it is far from a panacea.…In the future,* how *we educate children may prove more important than* how much *we educate them.…CQ + PQ > IQ.*

— T. L. Friedman (2006, pp. 302–303)

Several months ago, I finally muddled my way through Pulitzer Prize-winning author Thomas Friedman's bestselling *The World is Flat: A Brief History of the Twenty-First Century* (2006). It is, to say the least, a thought-provoking look at how the world has changed, is changing, and will change as a result of many forces, particularly technological advances. In moments of weakness, I find myself shamefully taking comfort in the fact that I am enough of a geezer that I can likely make it through the remaining years of my professional career without becoming completely obsolete. I worry, though, for my daughter and our students here at Edgewood. Are we preparing them for such a changing work environment? Can we even try? Should we? Friedman is equally stumped but has arrived at a few conclusions.

First, he suggests that in the future, the "right education" young people need will be less focused on specific courses and more concentrated on certain skills and attitudes. Several traits that, according to Friedman, will be important for anyone seeking to succeed in the future economy and are—somewhat surprisingly—not so cutting edge, after all. They include two that I detail below:

1. The most important ability students can develop is the ability to *learn how to learn*. These words likely sound familiar to teachers at our school. To succeed in the future workplace, students will need to

constantly absorb and teach themselves new ways to do old things and new ways to do new things. It will be not only what you know today, but how you learn that will set you apart. What courses should one take, then? According to Friedman: Go around to your friends and ask one question: "Who are your favorite teachers?" Make a list of those teachers and take those classes. It matters not if they are teaching Greek mythology, cooking, calculus, or American history. Thinking back on our favorite teachers, we know not the specifics of what they taught, but we sure remember being excited about learning it. What has stayed with us are not the facts they imparted but the excitement about learning they inspired. To learn how to learn, you have to love learning because so much learning is about being motivated to teach yourself. Which brings us to his second point that struck me…

2. *CQ + PQ > IQ.* This one is also affirming to many outstanding Edgewood teachers: *Curiosity Quotient plus Passion Quotient is greater than Intelligence Quotient.* In the flat world of which Friedman writes, educational opportunities are and will be pretty much limitless. Much of what you will ever need to know is out there on the Web. Paraphrasing Friedman: Give me a kid with a passion to learn and a curiosity to discover and I will take him any day over a less-passionate and less-curious kid with a high IQ, because curious, passionate kids are self-educators and self-motivators. They will always be able to learn. *Nobody works harder at learning than a curious kid.* If this is true, one of our primary goals as teachers should be to instill in students the quality of curiosity. The best way we can make kids love learning is to instill in them a sense of curiosity through our great teaching. As for passion, Friedman suggests that we cannot light the fire of passion in someone else if it does not burn within us first. If you love kids and can convey that, then even if you do not know your subject matter deeply, they will be inspired by you and they will learn beyond your classroom.

The two remaining skills Friedman advocates are *playing well with others* and *nurturing right-brain activity.* Again, these are very much unlike the bulk of his book in that they are a bit more "old school" ideas than futuristic visions. Yet, they remind us of our central charge, cultivating a community of passionate lifelong learners. Although his third and fourth points also made sense, the first two struck a chord in me for several reasons. First, I tend to agree that these will be the key to succeeding in the future economy. More importantly, though, they have *always* been the key to success. So, although we still need to continuously evolve and improve as educators, some things remain the same. Finally, I was struck by these two points of emphasis because it made me think that, at Edgewood, we are way ahead of most other schools in terms of excelling in these two important areas. It seems that we stress the importance of "learning how to learn" regularly. Moreover, we are adept at instilling curiosity and passion for learning within our students.

Taking a six-hundred-page book and imparting any of its wisdom in a page or two is a daunting—lo, futile—task, so I encourage you to take a look at Friedman's work yourself. I can state with certainty that if he were to visit Edgewood, he would find passion and curiosity in spades. The fact that our school is staffed with curious and passionate teachers is yet another example of how we *Teach with Passion* each day!

Have a curiously excellent weekend

Jeff

26

Response to Intervention Basics

What is Response to Intervention?

The reauthorized *Individuals With Disabilities Education Improvement Act* (IDEIA) of 2004 focuses on providing more effective instruction for *all* students by encouraging earlier intervention actions on the part of *all* educators for students experiencing academic or behavioral difficulties. Providing interventions through the use of a structured Response to Intervention (RTI) model can lead to significant changes in the way we teach all students, the way we respond when some students do not learn, and the way in which students with learning disabilities are identified. RTI is an assessment and intervention process for systematically monitoring student progress and making decisions about the need for instructional modifications or increasingly intensified services using progress monitoring data. RTI can also be defined as the practice of:

1. Providing high-quality instruction and interventions matched to student needs and…

2. Using learning rate over time and level of performance to…

3. Make important educational decisions. These three components of RTI are essential (NASDE, 2005).

Or to put it in an overly simple way, RTI is a systematic model designed to prepare *all* students to meet standards.

Although the RTI acronym has been floating around schools for several years now, very few teachers I have worked with seem to have a deep understanding of its purposes and components. Moreover, very few schools I have visited have implemented a comprehensive, coherent, consistent, and schoolwide RTI model. To some educators, RTI exists as another esoteric program that will soon go away. In reality, RTI is, by all indications, here to stay and its purposes are much simpler than many have been lead to believe.

What are the purposes of RTI? Ikeda, Rahn-Blakeslee, Niebling, Allison, and Stumme (2006) suggest four:

1. Looking at what we want and what we are getting.

2. Looking for an analysis of why problems occur.

3. Looking for the best way to intervene.

4. Looking for the best means of monitoring our progress and making decisions based on this monitoring.

Part of the difficulty in understanding RTI is that no one-size-fits-all model exists for implementing it. The federal government purposely provided few details for the implementation of RTI procedures, instead suggesting that state and local districts should be given the flexibility to establish models that reflect and best meet the needs of the communities they serve. Despite a certain amount of confusion surrounding RTI, it is clear that successful implementation of RTI will result in many benefits, including:

- Earlier identification of students who have learning or behavioral needs;

- Aligning assessment procedures with instructional practices;

- Providing multiple data points on which decisions are based;

- Using scientifically based instructional programs;

- Informed and involved parents who are better equipped to support and reinforce school interventions;

- Reduction in the over identification of minority students for special services;

- Promise for closing the achievement gap;

- Continuous school improvement model of assessing, planning, and implementing.

Although the potential benefits of RTI are many, much remains to be done at most schools to achieve full and effective implementation. Chief among the tasks facing educators leading RTI efforts is to make sure that every staff member has a clear understanding of each professional's role in the process. Classroom teachers—both regular education and special education—need to have a clear understanding of how RTI will work and will need to be trained in using diagnostic assessments, data analysis, and research-based strategic interventions. As with most change initiatives, the vital first step toward success centers on effective communication. Leaders at the district and school level need to communicate consistently and clearly what RTI is—and is not—what it will look like, and what it will require in the way of changes in current practices.

The Twenty-Sixth Friday

The following *Friday Focus* is one of the shortest ones included in this book. This brevity was intentional, as I was writing about a topic that very few teachers at our school—most schools?—had a deep understanding of or passion for. My goal was to keep this memo about RTI as simple as possible so that all teachers in the school would, first, be willing to take the time to read the entire writing and, second, be able to walk away with a "staring point" for understanding what RTI is all about. I knew that we had a great deal of work ahead of us in truly implementing an effective whole-school RTI program, and my goal was to formally begin this work by getting everyone to recognize the importance—and inevitability—of RTI. To be honest, at the time of this writing, RTI was not a deeply embedded component of our school's culture. Very few teachers embraced RTI as a framework for helping individual students who struggled academically or behaviorally, let alone as a whole-school strategy for ensuring high levels of learning for all students, starting with high-quality instruction at the tier 1 level: the general education classroom.

Although we are all overwhelmed with educational acronyms by this point, I created one more in the writing below in the hopes that this could be our school's starting point for building a common understanding of what RTI meant when condensed to its simplest form. It also had a bit of a silly ring to it, STIPCA, which I hoped teachers would recall in the days, months, and years ahead as we worked to make RTI a vital part of our school's culture. Although not a pretty-sounding acronym, STIPCA succinctly summarizes the very essence of RTI, which is all about Screening, Teaching, Intervening, Probing, Charting, and Adjusting. *Some* of the teachers at our school did *some* of these actions in a *somewhat* systematic manner at *some* time in the year. To truly impact our school culture, however, we needed to move from this random approach to RTI to a systematic, timely, directive, and school-wide approach.

Friday Focus!

RTI in and of itself is a movement—it's a decision that a school district makes to improve educational outcomes for all students, not just for those kids that struggle, but for all students.

> — Sheldon Horowitz, Director of Professional Services, National Center for Learning Disabilities (in Devaney, 2009)

As I mentioned at our staff meeting on Tuesday, Response to Intervention (RTI) is a movement in education that is a "have to," meaning all schools will be required to implement this in a systematic way, sooner rather than later. In my opinion, RTI is also a "must do," meaning it is so central to our core business that we must embrace this as something we actually *want* to do to ensure high levels of learning for all students.

RTI is intended to respond to individual students' needs—including those students falling behind as well as those not being challenged enough—by taking a data-based approach to instruction. In essence, RTI is a twofold system of reliable high-quality instruction and frequent formative assessment of student progress. Schools that are already succeeding in the area of RTI typically have in place six practices/actions as part of their RTI model. These actions are described below in a way that best addresses students who are not meeting expectations, but can also be adapted to address the needs of students exceeding expectations. I thought it might be helpful to list these six professional actions, providing a very brief explanation of each (These six actions can be memorized with the acronym STIPCA—a lame acronym, to be certain, but it may help you remember these RTI actions!).

Professional educators committed to RTI practices *will*…

1. *Screen:* Valid screening measures predict who is, and who is not, at risk for future learning difficulties. We primarily focus on the areas of reading and math when implementing RTI in schools and school districts. Effective screenings are characterized by quick, low-cost, repeatable testing of critical skills or behaviors (our Curriculum-Based Measurement work at the sixth grade level this year comes to mind).

2. *Teach:* Please recall that the single most important component of RTI is tier 1, where you will find the 80% figure in any RTI tier visuals you see. The better we do in teaching the core curriculum, the better we do at RTI! Teachers must be highly qualified (a given at our school) and deliver the stated curriculum as intended (you will often hear the phrase "…with fidelity to design/implementation" when reading about curriculum/instruction practices in an "RTI world").

3. *Intervene:* Providing "at-risk" students with enhanced opportunities to learn, including additional time exposed to the core curriculum in small groups, or supplementary instruction.

4. *Probe (Progress Monitoring):* Brief, frequent measures of specific skills to determine if students are responding to the interventions as intended.

5. *Chart:* Progress is regularly charted to provide a visual record of the actual rate of gain in specific skills in relation to a specific goal.

6. *Adjust:* Depending on whether the student is achieving a rate of progress determined by the specific goal, the manner and intensity of the intervention is adjusted.

These six action steps are a simple synopsis of what RTI is all about. RTI involves systematically evaluating the cause–effect relationship between an academic or behavioral intervention and a student's response to that intervention. The RTI model aligns with Professional Learning Community (PLC) principles in that it sets a foundation for collaboration among teachers—including "general ed" and "special ed" teachers—so that, together, we are focusing on "every ed." In addition, with the creation of intervention/extension blocks, RTI can serve as a vehicle for answering two of the four critical PLC questions: How will we respond when kids don't learn? and How will we respond when they have already learned the material? Working together to ensure that each child at our school has access to high-quality instruction and that struggling students are identified early and provided the interventions necessary to succeed is another way we *Teach with Passion* each day at our school!

Have an Awesome Weekend

Jeff

27

Principles of Great Teaching

The Twenty-Seventh Friday

In some ways, the following *Friday Focus* memo is another example of a "Book Review" *Friday Focus*, like those in Chapters 17 and 26. A key difference is that the book I mention at length in this writing—*Never Work Harder Than Your Students & Other Principles of Great Teaching* by Robyn Jackson (2009)—is actually a book written by an educator and intended for educators. Typically, when I reference a book that is directly applicable to our profession, my intent is to share specific strategies teachers can try in their classrooms, whereas, when I am writing a book review about a book not related to teaching, I am trying to show how what we do as educators parallels, impacts, and works in concert with what others are doing in different walks of life. In the following *Friday Focus*, I share two specific strategies teachers can use to get to know themselves and their students better. Also, although I do not present a detailed review of the entire book, I do share what the author suggests are seven principles of great teaching, principles that are hard to argue with and that I hoped all teachers would learn more about and embrace themselves.

Friday Focus!

Friday, March 7

The problem is not that we do not know enough—it is that we do not do what we already know. We do not act on or refine or apply those principles and practices that virtually every teacher already knows.

— Mike Schmoker (2006)

I have heard Schmoker speak on many occasions and would highly recommend two of his books, *Results: The Key to Continuous School Improvement* (1999) and *Results Now: How We Can Achieve Unprecedented Improvements in Teaching and Learning* (2006). What are these principles and practices of which Schmoker speaks in the quotation above that we should not just *know* but actually *do* as teachers? We could read fifty books on teaching and find fifty different such lists, I imagine (although we would likely find a good bit of commonality among the lot). Recently, I picked up a book just published by the Association for Supervision and Curriculum Development (ASCD), whose title piqued my interest: *Never Work Harder Than Your Students & Other Principles of Great Teaching* (2009) by Robyn R. Jackson. I enjoyed this book, in which Dr. Jackson shares her own list of effective teaching practices: *7 Principles of Mastery Teaching*. I find this to be an interesting book and thought it worthwhile to share her seven principles along with two practical suggestions she offers for fulfilling the first principle.

It goes without saying that our school is filled with master teachers. What is it that makes them so? Dr. Jackson suggests that, as master teachers, we should:

1. Start where our students are;

2. Know where our students are going;

3. Understand that expectations have more to do with us than they do with our students;

4. Use feedback to help our students get better at learning;

5. Be proactive;

6. Focus on quality rather than quantity; and

7. Never work harder than our students.

I found myself agreeing with much of what Jackson has to say in detailing each of these seven "master" teacher traits. Admittedly, principle #1 (start where your students are), is best read and applied at the beginning of the year, yet I found this chapter insightful and filled with practical ideas worthy of sharing, even at this point in the year. She suggests that we, as teachers, have "capital" (knowledge and skills) that we want our students to acquire. Our students, on the other hand, have widely varying "currencies" (knowledge and behaviors) that they attempt to use to acquire the capital of the classroom. Unfortunately, there is often a discrepancy between the currency we value and the currency they are spending. At times, we must reshape our approach to instruction so that we capitalize on our kids' currencies rather than negating or overriding them. Jackson suggests a strategy for examining our beliefs about what is acceptable in the classroom, what makes a "good student," and what constitutes learning. She also suggests using the "artifact bag" activity (Saphier & Gower, 1997) as a way of learning more about your students and creating a classroom culture that recognizes and values their various currencies.

- *Examining our Beliefs and Values:* Divide a piece of paper into two columns, listing on one side the behaviors and characteristics of your ideal student. What would the student know, do, look like, think? This list will show the currencies you value. Next, place an asterisk next to each characteristic that is necessary to master the standards of your course. On the other side, list the characteristics, values, and behaviors of the students in your class. What do they look like, act like, value? Compare the two lists to see the currencies you value and the currencies your students are spending. What are the similarities? Where are the disconnects? How many of the starred characteristics do your students already possess? What can you do to help your students acquire the starred characteristics they do not already have? The more we can observe and really listen to our kids, the more we can understand what they bring to the table and how we can capitalize on that to optimize the likelihood of their acquiring our capital.

- *Artifact Bag Activity:* Have students bring in an unlabeled shopping bag containing five items that represent their lives or interests. At various intervals throughout the first month of school, have a student select a bag at random and display the items one at a time. After the fifth item is shown, ask the class to make a collective guess as to its owner. Then, ask the bag's owner to explain the significance of each item.

Knowing our students means more than just knowing their overt classroom personas. We must delve deeper, striving to know the currencies they have and value, using that information to help them acquire the capital available in your classroom. Taking the time to really know our students and starting where they are is another way we *Teach with Passion* each day at Edgewood Middle School!

Happy Weekend!

Jeff

28

The Importance of Teaching Procedures

Pay Now, Save Later

Teaching classroom procedures takes time. A great deal of time. Whether we are talking about a first grade class or a twelfth grade honors English class, kids are kids and are, therefore, going to need constant instruction in terms of classroom procedural expectations. However, I have found that teachers who devote a great deal of time to approaching this somewhat mind-numbing task proactively, recoup this time as the year progresses, when they are no longer forced to behave reactively to students who are still not following classroom procedures and routines. In my younger years, I recall seeing an oil filter commercial on television hundreds of times. In this commercial the "mechanic" recommends changing one's oil filter regularly as a way to prevent more costly engine repairs down the line. The commercial always closed with this "mechanic" staring at me and stating ominously, "You can pay me now—or pay me later." Teaching procedures has something in common with this philosophy on automobile maintenance: we can pay attention to teaching our students these procedures at the outset or we can pay even more attention to it later.

In every school at which I have worked, I noticed that students actually enjoy an orderly classroom. Students perform better—both academically and behaviorally—when they know what is expected of them, not only in terms of the content they must master, but also the way in which they will behave, interact, and perform routine actions while in the class. Teachers who effectively teach and consistently enforce clear classroom procedures also prevent problems on those days when they are absent, as students are already well versed in what they are to do and how they are to behave. Wong and Wong (1998) observe that if teachers do not structure the classroom, students will structure the classroom for them. It goes without saying that presumably all teachers would prefer that this structure be left to them, rather than their students. Less obvious, perhaps, is the fact these very same students would also prefer that teachers take control of this aspect of the classroom. Wong and Wong (1998) suggest a three-step process for teaching classroom procedures to students:

1. Explain classroom procedures clearly.

2. Rehearse classroom procedures until they become routines.

3. Reinforce a correct procedure and re-teach an incorrect one.

As teachers, we should plan on spending a great deal of time at the beginning of each school year teaching procedures. We should continue to re-teach these procedures throughout the year, giving feedback to students as often as necessary. The more effectively we teach classroom procedures, the more content our students will ultimately learn.

The Twenty-Eighth Friday

As I mentioned in the introduction to this book, one year we decided to devote twenty-six editions of the weekly *Friday Focus* communication vehicle to an A to Z look at effective classroom instruction. The following *Friday Focus* is a writing from the week we were on the letter P and I decided to write about Procedures, something that is so important, yet so often overlooked, in planning for superior classroom instruction. Too often, teachers and administrators are so intently focused on the academic content they wish to convey to students that they fail to teach the routine procedures necessary for effectively and efficiently learning this content. I started off this writing by referencing our associate principal at the time, Matt Eriksen, and his family, including his newborn daughter, Ella. I used the fact that I was struggling to find the perfect baby gift for the Eriksens as a jumping off point for the important gifts that we, as teachers, give our students, including the gifts of "roots" and "wings."

I employed two analogies for stressing the relationship between teaching procedures and teaching content, suggesting that we must do both. Teaching procedures are compared to giving the gift of roots while teaching content is compared to giving the gift of wings. In addition, teaching procedures are compared to building the railroad tracks on which the "train" of content will run; the more we grease these *tracks of procedures*, the more efficiently our *trains of content* will run. If you were to observe for an entire class period at any grade level K–12, and consciously note all procedures that were employed throughout the lesson, you would likely find an enormous number of such procedures that students must master before, during, and after the actual lesson occurs. As teachers, we must avoid the temptation to assume that all students will simply pick up on our expectations for the many procedural actions we need them to master. Instead, we must build time into our lessons—throughout the school year—to teach, monitor, and reteach classroom procedures.

In this week's writing, I offer three examples of how teachers can reinforce procedural expectations (using the names of our school's three office workers to inject just a bit of humor). I also employ the "Eagle Idea" concept of sharing strategies I had seen teachers use in recent classroom observations that were effective ways of teaching classroom procedures to enhance learning. As I note below, Smith (2004) calls the teaching of procedures an invisible component to classroom management. Although it may be invisible when procedures are explicitly taught, in classrooms where procedures have not been taught, the results are very visible—and detrimental to student performance and teacher effectiveness.

Friday Focus!

Friday, March 21

There are two things we must give children: the first one is roots; the other, wings.

— Author Unknown

I devoted an inordinate amount of time this week trying to come up with a great gift for Ella Madelyn Eriksen...a stroller? diapers? a savings bond? several dozen expensive golf balls (this one was Matt's idea!)? All worthy ideas, perhaps, but no matter how creative or expensive my gift, it will pale in comparison to the gifts Erin and Matt will provide Ella, just as all parents who give so selflessly to their children. The tangible gifts we give our children are nice, but the intangible gifts of "roots" and "wings" are among the most important of all, gifts that loving parents give their children and loving teachers give their students. The "roots–wings" metaphor is an apt one not only for parents, but also for educators. At first glance, they seem to connote opposite ends of the spectrum: keep someone grounded while setting them free? Yet, we cannot accomplish the latter without first ensuring the former. In the classroom setting, the above quote can be applied on several levels to what we, as educators, endeavor to do in working with our students. One way that the roots–wings symbolism works is to picture the gift of roots as teaching our students behaviors that will increase their chances of success as we also give them wings—the freedom to make choices about their learning and their future. The more we can teach and promote positive behaviors now, the more likely we are grounding them in core values that will allow them to take flight later as they grow into productive and independent citizens.

In school, one way we teach behaviors is by teaching *procedures*. I feel that this is an often overlooked and important aspect of effective teaching. Unfortunately, it takes a great deal of time to teach procedures, yet I have always felt that this is time well spent and time that can be recouped later, as all kids learn precisely how to behave/proceed in any given situation. An obvious expert in this area of education is Harry Wong. Another is Rick Smith, whose book, *Conscious Classroom Management: Unlocking the Secrets of Great Teaching* (2004), I refer to often and who I have had the pleasure of hearing speak on many occasions. Rick refers to procedures as our "railroad tracks" with the curriculum/content being the "train." Once we clearly lay down the railroad tracks (*procedures*), the train (*content*) will run much more smoothly and in the right direction. In any K–12 classroom, there are a staggering number of procedures that must be taught. To list but a few, we must establish and teach procedures for the…

- Beginning of class
  - Students entering the classroom
  - Tardies/absences
  - Make up work
  - Beginning the lesson
  - Turning in/reviewing homework
- During class
  - Gaining student attention
  - Passing out papers
  - Headings on papers
  - Using the bathroom/water fountain/pencil sharpener
  - Turning in work
  - How students ask for help
  - Class discussions—raising hands
  - Group work
  - Watching videos
  - Student movement in the room
  - Taking tests and quizzes

- Ending class
  - Assigning homework
  - Dismissing class
  - Putting materials away
  - Cleaning the room

Again, these are but a cursory list of procedures that often arise and which must be taught in order to maximize limited instructional time each day.

Although we should and do spend more time at the outset of the year teaching procedures, Smith points out that we must reinforce procedural lessons throughout the school year and *recommends teaching at least two procedures every class period, regardless of what the lesson is* (e.g., "Thanks, Barb, for answering that in a nice loud voice we could all hear." or "Angela, thank you for raising your hand; what is your question?" or "Aaron, remember to keep your head up when we watch a video."). Sadly, research shows that more middle school students can spell "Budweiser" than "Eisenhower." Smith suggests that this is because while they may learn about Eisenhower once a year, they are regularly bombarded with 15- or 30-second Budweiser messages. Although not an ideal message for kids in this instance, we can learn from such advertising techniques. Don't forget to include these spot-check "Budweisers" throughout the school year in order to grease the procedural tracks on which our content is delivered.

Rick often tells a story about his preteaching experience when he observed several teachers in action. He soon realized that when some teachers asked students to "turn to page 27" all students immediately and quietly did so. When other teachers asked the very same thing, some students turned to page 27, some asked what page they were to turn to, some asked if they could go get their book, some opened the wrong book, and some complained or talked loudly while rummaging through a book bag. At first, Smith could not discern what made the difference and came to realize that effective classroom management is essentially invisible. He later classified his theory of *invisible classroom management* (2004) into three categories: (a) *foundation;* (b) *prevention;* and (c) *intervention.* Teaching procedures fall into the "prevention" category and still makes a great deal of sense to me as time well spent. I hope to elaborate more on Rick Smith's good work and his specific tips in a later *Friday Focus,* but I thought of Rick's emphasis on teaching procedures Monday when I was in Kathleen's amazing math classroom. Her kids were doing something I have seen them do before and they always do this in a completely orderly, organized, efficient, and work-oriented way. What they were doing was nothing too out of the ordinary; they were simply using personal white board slates to scribble down, complete, and display math problems. Yet, they did it so smoothly and orderly that it was clear Kathleen had outlined—however briefly—the procedures for doing so. In addition, she likely "Budweisers" them each time she has them use these white slates.

There are a zillion other examples ("Eagle Ideas": Julie's science lab procedures; Sara's Book Review Groups; Mikki's red-green-yellow cards that student groups use to show their response) I could cite of Edgewood teachers teaching procedures effectively. Taking time to lay these procedural railroad tracks is how we give "roots" to our students. Having grounded them in this way, they can more readily grasp the academic content, growing the "wings" that will take them to new heights each day. Giving the gifts of roots and wings to our kids each day is yet another example of how we *Teach with Passion* each day!

Have an awesome weekend; this one's for you!

Jeff

29

A Culture of Change

The Thirty-First Friday

In this week's *Friday Focus*, I write at length about change. One reason I chose this topic at this point in the school year is because teachers were already looking ahead to the following school year and beginning to worry about a few inevitable changes that they were already learning about, both at the district and school levels. As educators, we are in a constant state of change. Truthfully, though, in talking to many friends in many other walks of life, it appears that these folks are equally immersed in careers fraught with change and upheaval. Still, school leaders must continue to honestly confront the topic of change, communicating with staff what is and is not changing, explaining why change is occurring and how it will impact all school stakeholders. In the writing below, I draw upon an observation of Fullan's (2008) to make several points: the key to successful change depends on what teachers do and think.

In thinking about change and reflecting on many teachers I have known who embraced change and many more who resisted change of any kind, I have come to realize that, although it is indeed necessary to communicate clearly about any and all anticipated changes, it is also true that, in the end, we will not convince everyone that the planned changes are for the better. In such instances, we need to focus on changing teacher behaviors, if not their beliefs. Oftentimes, teachers who begin by changing their behaviors ultimately end up changing their beliefs. To put it another way, it is much more realistic to expect people to *act* themselves into a new way of *thinking* than it is to *think* themselves into a new way of *acting*.

Change is real and can be real scary. To begin this *Friday Focus* dedicated entirely to change, I offer a humorous quote about change to set the stage for a lighter approach. I also write at some length about a sampling of many things that we knew would absolutely *not* be changing in the foreseeable future, most of which were of paramount importance to our school culture. Finally, I close by asking teachers to watch a very short film clip on the topic of change. I encourage all readers to also watch this excellent video as well as other similarly inspiring and insightful video clips and resources found at www.simpletruths.com.

Friday Focus!

Friday, March 28

Change is good….you go first.

— Anderson & Feltenstein (2009)

My topic for this *Friday Focus* originated after reading Matt's Eriksen's e-mail, in which he mentioned transformation and change in schools. As one who actually enjoys change, this is an area of research that fascinates me and of which I have read voluminously in recent years. After all this reading and research, I arrive conflicted in that I am not certain whether schools are changing too much—or too little. Although we face continuous change in District 112 and Edgewood, one change expert I respect once told me that we should begin the change process by discussing what *isn't* changing.

At Edgewood next year, we can count on many changes, yet so much more remains the same. First and foremost, our mission remains the same and we will continue to nurture, empower, and inspire each and every Edgewood Eagle. Our hours will be the same, our schedule will be the same, our student demographics will be very similar, and the fact that we will be teaching some of the finest middle school students in the state will not change. Our staff will be almost identical to this year, nearly all of our current sixth and seventh grade students will return, our lunch program and after school activities will remain almost unchanged, we will have the same number of extended advisory sessions, and we will teach the same number of students for the same number of minutes throughout the year. Our academic calendar year will be a mirror image of the current year, our curriculum resources will be much the same, the support that we receive from parents will remain the same, our employment benefits will remain the same or better, our facility will not change dramatically, our student–teacher ratio will not change, and our student arrival and dismissal procedures will not change. One could go on, of course, but you get my point. Moreover, some of the changes we *will* face are merely differences, rather substantive changes. For example, we will have a new associate principal next year, which will be *different*. Yet, we will have an amazing, hardworking, intelligent, and passionate associate principal in place next year, which is *no change* at all from the current situation.

Having said all this, I realize, of course, that we do face continuous change in our profession, both of the unimportant and significant variety. To implement change successfully, I defer to all that Michael Fullan has to say on the topic. First and foremost, *he suggests that effective school change depends on what teachers do and think—it is as simple and as complex as that.* Effective teachers account for 30% of the variance in student learning and real pupil improvement comes from the power of having three good teachers in a row (Fullan, 2008). Fullan maintains that the best way to effect positive change in teachers throughout the school is to create cultures focused on results, learning, and collaboration. Because teachers are the ones with the greatest impact on student learning, we must work together and learn together to achieve organizational knowledge creation:

- People must work together to figure out what is needed to achieve that which is worthwhile.

- You cannot get internal commitment and ingenuity from outside—expertise lies within.

- The only problems worth solving are the ones that exist within each and every organization.

- Change is forever: Problems don't stay solved, so we have to learn to do the right thing over and over again.

Schools with positive, productive cultures constantly worry about what is worthwhile and how to get there. They continually convert tacit knowledge into explicit shared ideas.

Despite my intermittent fear that schools across our great nation are actually not changing enough, I never want to underestimate the anxiety, uncertainty, and fear that impending change can cause within many. We must learn to live with change, of course. We must learn to take change both less and more seriously at the same time. Less, because most change is superficial; more, because it is important to sift through the nonessential change until we breakthrough to real change: shared meaning, commitment, and improvement. Fullan believes that the best defense against a seemingly relentless pace of change is to build professional learning communities that excel at sorting out the worthwhile from the nonworthwhile.

In closing, please take three minutes to watch this great clip on the topic of change, based on the book by Anderson and Feltenstein (2009). I enjoy many of their twenty-one principles relating to change, in particular: (a) *Forget Success:* it's easier for organizations to come up with new ideas than to let go of old ones; (b) *Focus on Strengths:* focus on the critical few, not the inconsequential many; (c) *Inspire Personal Accountability:* I always wondered why somebody didn't do something about that. Then, I realized I was somebody; (d) *Celebrate Success:* compensation is a right; recognition is a gift; and (e) *Follow Your Con-*

victions: some focused on what was—others what could be, but—together—they made it happen.

http://www.changeisgoodmovie.com/

Accepting that we will always be faced with numerous inconsequential changes as well as a few potentially significant changes is necessary for our sanity. Recognizing how to ignore the former and learning to embrace the latter is yet another way that we *Teach with Passion* each day at our school!

Have an Awesome Weekend, as we **Change** from March to April!

Jeff

30

Reinforcing Effort

The Thirtieth Friday

I am particularly pleased to include the next two *Friday Focus* writings in this book. Both were written by Chuck Bell, a principal who began the practice of writing and sharing weekly *Friday Focus* memos after reading my first book, *Improving Your School One Week at a Time* (2006). Since that time, Chuck and I have exchanged *Friday Focus* memos on a regular basis and I always learn a great deal from reading his insightful and well-written communications to his staff at Commerce Middle School, where he has served as principal for several years. Commerce Middle School is located in northeast Georgia, approximately twenty miles from Athens, Georgia, home to The University of Georgia. The school Chuck serves as principal includes just over 500 students in grades 6 to 8, many of whom come from diverse backgrounds, including an economically disadvantaged population that stands at well over 50%. When Chuck arrived at Commerce Middle School, test scores were at a point that the school was not making the grade in terms of Adequate Yearly Progress (AYP) status. One year after arriving as principal at the school, test scores improved dramatically and Commerce Middle School made AYP. Chuck will credit the hard work of his students and staff to this success, but having worked with him and getting to know him over the past two years, it is clear that his leadership in changing the school's culture played a key role in the school's success.

This first of Chuck's two *Friday Focus* writings included in this book is an apt one for Commerce Middle School—and for any school: the importance of effort and its impact on one's achievement. The story of Commerce Middle School's recent achievement gains is a testament to the powerful impact that effort has upon outcomes. Ironically, if we were to poll every educator in the nation, asking them what led to their success as a professional educator, I would hazard to guess that very few, if any, would attribute their success to an extremely high IQ, or the tremendous scores they earned on the SAT, or the 4.0 grade-point average they carried in high school or college. Instead, the vast majority of educators would likely attribute a great deal of their success to the hard work they put in over time toward achieving their goals. Chuck suggests that we keep this in mind with the students we teach. Although we must always hold kids accountable for mastering standards, ultimately assigning grades and administering standardized tests to measure "ability," we must also find ways to recognize, encourage, and reward student effort.

Chuck's *Friday Focus* below makes an eloquent and powerful case that a direct correlation exists between effort and achievement and that we, as educators, must find ways to encourage effort within all students. He closes his weekly memo by providing additional resources for teachers seeking more information related to effort-based ability.

Friday Focus!

Friday, April 4

Despite the beliefs of most Americans about the importance of working hard to succeed in life, many educational approaches are still constructed on what may be called an "innate ability paradigm." Overemphasis of innate abilities often results in children formulating estimates of their own capacity to learn, and creating doubt about their ability to succeed in many learning tasks (especially when the task is advertised as being difficult).

This approach or belief system comes into direct conflict with our goal that all students can and should be expected to work toward and learn the same high standards. If we are to truly embrace this goal/belief, we must shift our attention toward more effort-based approaches. Research makes clear the connection between effort and achievement—believing you can, often makes it so. Because students may not be aware of the importance of believing in effort, teachers should explicitly teach and exemplify the connection between effort and achievement.

Students who make this connection recognize that effort is something they can control. When students attribute success to ability, luck, or task difficulty, they are less likely to exert effort and take ownership over their learning. However, when students attribute their success to effort, this can translate into a willingness to engage in and complete a task. Students' beliefs and attitudes have a significant effect on their success or failure in school.

Students need multiple opportunities to succeed. Success leads to efficacy and efficacy to esteem. As the work of David Perkins (1995) and Lauren Resnick (2001) shows, strategies, ability, confidence, and acceleration help produce effective effort which leads to achievement.

Thanks to all for taking the time to consider this important aspect of student learning. Below are some resources that shed more light on this subject for those of you interested in learning more about the relationship between effort and achievement:

- Not all students know the connection between effort and achievement (Seligman, 1990, 1994; Urdan, Migley, & Anderman, 1998).

- Student achievement can increase when teachers show the relationship between an increase in effort and an increase in success (Craske, 1985; Van Overwalle & De Metsenaere, 1990).

- Rewards for accomplishment can improve achievement when the rewards are directly linked to successful attainment of an understood performance standard (Cameron & Pierce, 1994).

- http://www.netc.org/focus/strategies/rein.php

Happy Weekend!

Chuck Bell

31

Test Preparation

The Thirty-First Friday

What follows is the second of two *Friday Focus* writings included in this book that were written by Chuck Bell, principal at Commerce Middle School in Commerce, Georgia. Chuck sent this *Friday Focus* memo to his staff on the Friday before the annual CRCT exams—the State of Georgia's AYP accountability tests—were to be administered. The title of this chapter is "Test Preparation," but at this point in the school year, Chuck was not writing about how we prepare students for testing in terms of teaching curriculum materials; instead, he was writing about how educators can prepare their students—and themselves—mentally for the tests so as to enhance optimal performance.

This *Friday Focus* nicely parallels Chuck's previous writing in that both focus on subordinating in importance any discrete, innate ability to a trait that is equally, if not more important. In the previous chapter, that trait was effort. In this memo, that trait is confidence. We can give our students and each other no greater gift than the gift of confidence. Students who believe they can perform well usually do. Teachers who have confidence in their abilities to teach and inspire students to succeed are often able to do so. In this writing, Chuck, as principal, extends this gift of confidence to his teachers and reminds them to pay it forward to their students. In addition, he does not merely "cheerlead" his teachers as they prepared to administer these important tests, he offers specific and effective strategies they can use in their classrooms to increase the likelihood that students would perform well. At the time of this *Friday Focus*, teachers had spent the better part of eight months preparing students by teaching them academic content; now it was time to prepare them how best to show all that they had learned during this time.

Friday Focus!

Friday, April 11

At Commerce Middle School, we often talk about leaving nothing to chance in our efforts to improve student achievement. With two school days remaining until we begin CRCT testing, I have reflected a great deal on the quality of teaching and learning that has taken place at our school this year. Our focused plans of improvement and ongoing efforts to assess and monitor the performance of our students and ourselves have resulted in a level of unquestionable readiness. It is with great confidence that I can exclaim, "We are ready!"

Beyond the test administration procedures discussed at this Wednesday's general faculty meeting, it is essential that on CRCT test days, our school (and individual classroom) environments be positive and upbeat, while maintaining a businesslike approach to the task at hand. It will serve us well to give attention to the smallest of details throughout the testing periods. You know your students very well. From test-anxious students to those who seem to be less than focused, please be prepared to work positively through issues in a situational fashion. What works with one student may have little or no effect on another. Group-wise, powerful phrases such as "You are prepared," or "I believe in you" are sure to have a positive impact on any student. Thank you for avoiding topics that have negative connotations, such as "If you fail this test, you may not be promoted."

We have talked a great deal about test-taking tips and strategies; as a result of your work with students, they will be able to approach each exam in a "test-wise" manner. Keep in mind that your classroom environment can be optimized in many ways. Instructional materials that may prompt student responses should not be visible in your classrooms. But please remember that your room is full of concealed information that should remain in place. Leave your concept maps and instructional posters up, but simply turn them around so that the printed information is not visible. Suggest to your students that they may visualize what was on the boards and walls to trigger their memories. Tell them also that *you* are covered with invisible information and that they can look at you and remember the concepts and skills you shared with them.

Sitting in any chair for more than a short interval is likely to have negative effects on anyone. I strongly recommend that you engage your students in movement at appropriate times during the testing periods. As a minimum, have them stand and stretch a bit before beginning their test, and have them move around during the break. If you want to take it a step further, have them take part in some arm or leg crossover activities that force both hemispheres of the brain to "talk" to each other. "The left arm pats the right shoulder" or "Pat your head and rub your belly." Other activities may include marching in place while patting opposite knees, or touching opposite elbows or heels.

Lastly, thank you in advance for continuing to emphasize the time factor on each test day. There is more than enough time for every student to fully complete each of the CRCT tests. We don't need any speed-testers! With the time that is allotted, students should be using the strategies you've taught them to review and rank questions (☺, +, ?), and should be double-checking all answers, especially on the questions they considered to be easy. Above all, remind them that *just having a strategy is important* and that effectively using the strategy can make a big difference for them. I will also reemphasize next week in my announcements that, "It is okay to be the last one done!"

Regardless of how we feel about standardized tests—what they measure and don't measure, or their deficiencies or consequences—as educators, we are obliged to do what is necessary to prepare our students for the tests. You have done a remarkable job in doing exactly that! With confidence, *you* can exclaim, "WE ARE READY!"

Have a great weekend!

Chuck Bell

32

Team Values

The Thirty-Second Friday

The following *Friday Focus* is another resulting from our A to Z series of *Friday Focus* writings that we undertook as a theme one year. Although most of these writings were focused on issues relating directly to classroom instruction, for the letter T, I seized the opportunity to write about teamwork. Although it may not be directly related to classroom instruction, it is a critical component to the success of any classroom—and any school. Building positive *classroom* cultures is every bit as important as creating and maintaining positive *schoolwide* cultures. A critical foundation of a positive classroom or school culture is effective teamwork.

Effective teams are a hallmark of effective schools. To create and maintain high-performing teams, all members of the team must share and adhere to similar commitments, or values. Moreover, they must understand what their mission is and share a vision for what they can become. They must set commonly agreed upon goals, and hold each other accountable for attaining them. In the following communication, I write about teamwork and how the concepts of mission, vision, values, and goals help to strengthen teams. I begin by sharing another excellent resource from the folks at www.simple-truths.com. The messages conveyed in this brief video clip aligned perfectly with what our school's leadership team had been working on in terms of revisiting and creating statements of mission, vision, and values, which we intended to use in guiding our work toward improving our school during the remainder of the school year as well as in future years.

Teamwork and school culture go hand in hand; show me a school, grade level, or academic department operating as an effective team, with all members aware of and dedicated to common mission, vision, value, and goal statements, and I will show you a school, grade level, or academic team with a positive culture, making a difference in the lives of the students they serve and each other. After sending this *Friday Focus* memo out via e-mail and posting on our school's wiki page, several staff members responded that they enjoyed the video so much that they, in turn, shared it with students in their classes, discussing teamwork and how important it is to success in any venture.

Friday Focus!

T is for Teamwork

Without shared values, peak performance is not possible....[S]uccess occurs when qualified people align on a common objective....[M]aking the team means doing what it takes to fulfill the mission....[E]ach member has a role in the team's success....[W]hen each team member accepts full responsibility and strives for excellence, trust and performance increase exponentially and the team is ready to take off.

— The Power of Teams

In reading the quote above, excerpted from the www.simpletruths.com film clip referenced below, one might hazard a guess as to what type of team they are directed: a sports team? A Fortune 500 company? A governmental agency? Maybe even a school, or a classroom within a school? In truth, these quotes apply to any effective team within any effective organization. Although they are universal in their wisdom about and application for high-performing teams, in this instance, I excerpted them from a book and accompanying film clip relating to one of the most successful and enduring teams of all time: The Blue Angels. Take a minute and watch this clip (it only takes two minutes!):

http://www.powerofteamworkmovie.com/

This clip is from Simple Truths, a company whose products I have enjoyed from time to time and which relate to organizational effectiveness and are founded on one simple truth: that less is always more. When I came across this clip recently, we had just finished talking about professional learning communities (PLCs) at our Leadership Team meeting. Hal Schmeisser led a discussion on a chapter of the book we are studying. This chapter contains many great ideas, but is primarily centered on what are known as the four foundations of a PLC: *Mission, Vision, Values,* and *Goals.* In a nutshell, a *Mission* is a statement of purpose: *Why do we exist?* A *Vision* is a glimpse toward our future: *What do we want to become? Values* are the commitments to which we agree and that will help us accomplish our mission: *How will we behave so that we can realize our vision?* Finally, *Goals* are the targets and timelines we establish regularly to ensure we are moving toward our dream: *How will we regularly mark our progress?* (DuFour, DuFour, Eaker, & Many, 2006).

For those of us who have been around awhile, mission statements and vision statements may seem like tiresome, irrelevant practices. We have seen them created before with great fanfare only to be quickly forgotten. However, I firmly believe that these statements—agreed upon by consensus, communicated regularly, and enforced consistently—are indispensable to achieving optimal levels of performance for all within a learning organization. I encourage you to consider the four cornerstones of PLCs: mission, vision, values, and goals (M, V, V, G). Consider these not only from a schoolwide perspective, but also from a personal perspective. Take a moment to reflect on your purpose for being here at our school. What is your foremost role as an educator? What would you like to be known for as a teacher? How must you act in order to succeed? What are your short-term targets?

When a large team of committed professionals individually establish clearly defined statements of M, V, V, G and collectively agree to a few overarching ones as an entire staff, the possibilities for student, teacher, and school success are unlimited. Although we may not literally soar through the upper altitudes like the Blue Angels, we will assuredly achieve new heights each and every year. Defining with a laser-like focus our purpose, our dreams, our ideal behaviors, and our short-term targets are four critical ways that we *Teach with Passion!* at our school.

Happy Weekend

Jeff

33

A Culture of Learning, Laughing, Loving

The Thirty-Third Friday

The following *Friday Focus* is one I wrote, but is nearly a "guest author" version in that I borrowed much of the contents—including the opening quotation—from a former colleague, Garry Puetz. At the time of this writing, I had moved from serving as a principal in Georgia to serving as a principal in Illinois, but I still kept in touch with many friends and former colleagues in Georgia. As I mention in the writing below, Garry was our school system's transportation director. As such, he did not necessarily possess a ton of expertise relating to the most pressing teaching and learning issues facing educators, but he certainly knew a great deal about creating and maintaining positive cultures in schools—or any workplace. According to Garry, positive cultures are built upon three Ls: *Learning, Laughing,* and *Loving*. Although I had served as a school administrator for many years, this was my first year serving as principal at this particular school and I wanted to communicate as often as possible my hope that we would exist as a school in which all teachers and all students *learned* continuously, *laughed* often, and *loved* each other as well as the work in which we were engaged.

This *Friday Focus* is not based on any scientific research and requires little in the way of any introduction, but in rereading it just now, I am reminded why I was moved to write and share it at this time with our staff. First, we were entering the final month of school and we had a lot going on, as most schools do at this time of year. Teacher stress levels seemed to be at an all-time high. I was so busy myself that I had returned to school on a Thursday evening to write the *Friday Focus* for the next day. As I mention in the memo, I entered our front lobby and discovered that Mr. White's classroom had been moved in its entirety—desks, chairs, wall decorations, trash cans, flag, everything—to the front office lobby. A teacher who was also working late passed by and told me that some of Mr. White's students had moved everything out of the classroom and into the lobby as a practical joke on their teacher—a man they liked and respected a great deal. I immediately started laughing and felt better about my personal workload as well as our school's climate and culture—I wanted to work at a school in which teachers and students had fun while working and learning together. Unfortunately, the teacher who I was laughing with then told me that one of our veteran teachers had also seen this as she was leaving for the day and commented angrily that it was inappropriate and that the joking between this teacher and his students had gone too far. I was disappointed that this particular teacher would have this reaction. At the same time, I was happy that she had given me an idea for the *Friday Focus* that I needed to write that evening.

I certainly recognize that as professional educators we must be careful about not offending anyone through our attempts at humor and that what is funny to one person is not necessarily funny to another. However, in this particular case, I felt that our kids had cleverly—and appropriately—delivered just what we needed at a tense point in the school year, and I wanted to subtly communicate to our teachers that this was something to be welcomed, not feared. As a followup, that Friday was a delight. Mr. White spent the first part of the day teaching his classes in the front lobby before having his students help him move everything back into his classroom after lunch. Students throughout the school got a good-natured laugh when they arrived that morning, and many teachers made it a point to visit this new "classroom" during the morning smiling and laughing at what they saw.

Friday Focus!

Friday, April 25

A key characteristic of effective teachers and leaders: they learn*…about themselves, about others, and about their job.*

— Garry Puetz

Wow! It is hard to believe that we have reached the point in the school year when we have but a handful of Fridays remaining! We have had an awesome year of teaching and learning thus far, and I want to thank each and every staff member for the friendship and support you have shown me in my first year as principal at our school. As the quote above suggests, learning is a key to success and I have learned many things about our school this year. This quote is not from anyone immediately recognizable to most, I am sure, although if you Google his name you will likely find that he played in the NFL for a dozen or so years awhile ago. Yet, I know Garry not from his playing days; instead, he was the director of transportation in my previous school system and one of our system's most recognized leaders. Each year, at our school's quarterly ceremonies recognizing student excellence, I would ask a speaker to come and say a few words to our kids about success. Garry came once each year and inevitably talked about the three Ls that he felt helped him succeed in life: *Learn, Laugh,* and *Love.*

I often steal these words of advice when talking to young people on such occasions as graduation. Regardless of our age or our station in life, to succeed, we must continually *learn:*

> *Supposing is good, but finding out is better.*
>
> — Mark Twain

> *We shall not cease from exploration, and the end of all our exploring will be to arrive where we started, and to know the place for the first time.*
>
> — T. S. Eliot

Successful people also *laugh* a lot. They laugh at themselves and with others. Even at this time of the school year, when everything seems so hectic that I have to come back to school at 8:00 P.M. to create the FF and catch up on everything else I did not get to today, I recall many good laughs I have enjoyed with you recently. From returning to school last evening, only to see Jason White's entire classroom transported to the front lobby by his practical-joking students, to watching so many of you have fun with the "Oh, the Places You'll Go" video, to having Kathleen McGrath utter yet another "punny" remark in front of her class, having good, wholesome fun with our students—who like us more and respect us more for doing so—makes our school a better place in which to teach and learn.

> *Against the assault of laughter, nothing can stand.*
>
> — Mark Twain

> *Gentlemen, why don't you laugh? With the fearful strain that is upon me day and night, if I did not laugh I should die, and you need this medicine as much as I do.*
>
> — Abraham Lincoln, during the Civil War

Finally, we need to *love.* We need to love *what we do*, love *why we do it*, and love *who we do it with*—our kids and each other.

> *When you fish for love, bait with your heart, not our brain.*
>
> — Mark Twain

> *Do what you love. Know your own bone; gnaw at it, bury it; unearth it, and gnaw it still.*
>
> — Henry David Thoreau

So, with apologies for blatant plagiarizing of my former colleague, I share with you his seemingly simple keys to success and thank you for embodying them all the year long and for learning, laughing, and loving each and every minute that we have remaining this year with our kids and with each other:

> Know less; Learn more…
> Worry less; Laugh more…
> Fear less; Love more…
> …And all the good things are yours.

Serving as teachers who *learn, laugh,* and *love* are three major ways that we *Teach With Passion* each day at our school!

Have an Awesome Weekend!

Jeff

34

Teacher Appreciation

The Thirty-Fourth Friday

Each year, during Teacher Appreciation Week, I struggle to come up with a way to show our teachers just how much I value all that they do to make our school a better place in which to teach and learn. Typically, neither our school budget nor my personal bank account has nearly enough available funds to purchase extravagant gifts for every teacher at the school. Although I always do find a way to provide some type of small gift and provide a breakfast or lunch for teachers during the week, I also make it a point to express my appreciation at the end of Teacher Appreciation Week through the *Friday Focus* memo.

In the *Friday Focus* that follows, I purposely keep the length very short, although I direct teachers to watch an inspiring video that serves as a vivid and compelling example of the powerful influence we have as teachers. Several teachers at my school thanked me for the small gifts we provided them during this week; many more wrote to thank me for sharing this video with them. Take a moment to watch this yourself at the link below.

Friday Focus!

Friday, May 2

I have the ability to reach out and touch someone in a positive way that will result in a product that's gonna make a better world for some other people in some other place at some point in the future.

— Albert Siedlecki, Teacher

For this week's *Friday Focus*, I will show my true appreciation by not making you read as many words as I typically do! However, I do hope you can take five minutes to view the attached video clip. I came across it last night when I was researching "teacher appreciation" and it really touched me, reminding me of so many Edgewood teachers. The clip is about a middle school science teacher in New Jersey (quoted above) and the profound impact he had on a student who went on to become an accomplished neurosurgeon, Dr. Lee Buono.

Dr. Buono indicates that the main reason he decided to pursue a career as a neurosurgeon is because his middle school science teacher told him one day after school that he had that potential within him, stating, "My teacher, who I respected, told me that I had what it took to become a brain surgeon!" Watching this clip, I am reminded of the profound influence you have in the lives of your current students, many of whom will call you years hence, thanking you for believing in them today, so they could grow to become successful surgeons, lawyers, teachers, engineers, and bankers later in life. You are molding the future each day, just as Albert Siedlecki has apparently been doing for 40 years as a middle school teacher in New Jersey.

Although I am supremely confident that all of your current students will look back as adults and sincerely appreciate all that you did to help them succeed, I suspect that some of them either do not appreciate that impact at the present time or, if they do, are not always willing to let you know their feelings. Therefore, let me thank you on their behalf; although Mr. "Si" seems like an amazing teacher, we have a host of equally gifted and inspirational teachers right here at Edgewood. I hope you have had a great week and I thank you for all your efforts throughout the year. Finding the unique talents within each of our students and letting them know that we have confidence in their abilities and their future are two more ways we *Teach With Passion* each day at our school! Enjoy this short video:

http://www.youtube.com/watch?v=xFs8P_TrAVQ

Have an Awesome Weekend!

Jeff

35

It's All About You...

The Thirty-Fifth Friday

The final three *Friday Focus* writings in this book are three of the very last ones I wrote as principal at a middle school where I had served for four years. During that time, I had written approximately 100 such memos and other teachers and leaders in our school or district had written an additional forty or so. Although I was excited about moving on to a new phase in my professional career, I was also sad to be leaving a school that exhibited one of the most positive school cultures imaginable and a school that had received a tremendous amount of recognition at the local, state, and national levels for superior student achievement and teacher performance. The following *Friday Focus* is another in our A to Z series; for the letter Y, I wrote about one of the cornerstones of our school's culture, something I referred to as the "You variable." I use this term to communicate my core belief that the single greatest variable related to student success is the quality of each student's teacher or teachers. Similarly, the single most important characteristic of a great school is that it is staffed by great teachers. Regardless of where we teach or what grade level or subject area we teach, we can be certain that we will be faced with many obstacles on a daily basis. How we respond to such obstacles determines the extent to which we will succeed.

During the final several weeks of the school year, I tend to use the *Friday Focus* to write in a way that—I hope—inspires and motivates teachers, making them feel affirmed about the work they have accomplished throughout the year without looking too far ahead to the next school year or trying to share a host of new strategies to implement in the classroom. In this *Friday Focus*, one of my main goals is simply to encourage teachers, and I reference one of my favorite leadership books, *Encouraging the Heart* (Kouzes & Posner, 2003), as one tool to achieve my purpose. In encouraging teachers at our school, I highlight several characteristics of our culture which were widely recognized as being solidly in place throughout the entire school at this point in time. First and foremost among them was our belief that the single most important classroom variable was "You"—the classroom teacher.

Friday, May 9

Y is for *you!*

Really believe in your heart of hearts that your fundamental purpose, the reason for being, is to enlarge the lives of others. Your life will be enlarged also. And all of the other things we have been taught to concentrate on will take care of themselves.

— Pete Thigpen (Executive Reserves Consulting Firm)

I have enjoyed each of the A to Z lessons about teaching and learning that we have shared with each other throughout this school year. For the letter Y, I wanted to write about the most important variable in determining the success of any student or any school: *You.*

You are absolutely the most important factor within your classroom in terms of determining to what extent your kids will learn, behave, and adjust socially and emotionally throughout the year. Collectively, *we* are the most important factor determining how well all 910 of our students will perform during a given year. Although *you* are the most important variable, that does not mean other factors do not play a role. Indeed, family demographics, poverty rates, home life situations, and English language ability are but a few variables that impact a student's and a school's level of success. Based on all variables, we may not be able to have the highest CRCT scores of any middle school in the State of Georgia. However, what the *You variable* does mean is that we have the power to take our kids from where they arrive and take them to levels of academic, social, and emotional well-being that teachers at other schools may not be able to match.

Recently, I have been reading a book by two of my favorite authors who have written several volumes on organizational leadership. One of their most recent is called *Encouraging the Heart* (Kouzes & Posner, 2003). Although it is a book written primarily for corporate leaders, I think that almost all of its wisdom applies to the school setting as well. Its central theme—encouraging the hearts of those with whom we interact at work—is one that, in my opinion, is a reason the *You variable* is so widely recognized as a key to our success here at Otwell. "Going the extra mile" is not merely a cliché at our school; it is the way we conduct our business on a regular basis. According to Kouzes and Posner, there are seven behaviors that leaders practice in order to "encourage the heart." Read through them and see if these are not the very same behaviors that Otwell Middle School teachers engage in, which, again, makes our *You variable* that much more powerful than our colleagues at surrounding schools:

1. Set clear standards
2. Expect the best
3. Pay attention
4. Personalize recognition
5. Tell the story
6. Celebrate together
7. Set the example

Hopefully, we follow these guidelines as a whole school in terms of working with each other professionally. More importantly, I know that individual teachers at our school follow these in working with their students each day. It is what sets our teachers apart and allows us to reach levels of performance that our demographics would suggest we should not be reaching.

At every school in America, there are students who sometimes misbehave. There are students who sometimes fail a test and there are students who at times will fail to complete their work. These are not really variables, then. The variable is how we respond when these student outcomes occur. At Otwell Middle School, our *You variable* kicks in and we do whatever it takes to relearn the material, or improve the behavior, or afford the student a second opportunity to complete an assignment—in other words, we encourage the heart.

Demographics are very real and they do impact student and school success. In my four years at Otwell, however, I have come to learn something that I hold onto as one of my most steadfast educational beliefs: Superior teaching trumps "difficult" demographics—or any other challenge we might face. The master teachers who staff our school have taught me this lesson loud and clear. *You* are the reason our kids succeed at school—at levels higher than they would had they attended another school with less passionate, encouraging teachers. Accepting that we stand as our students' most important variable in terms of their school success and acting in ways which encourage the heart are examples of how we commit to *Teaching with Passion* at our school each day!

Happy Weekend!

Jeff

36

...But It's Not About You at All!

The Thirty-Sixth Friday

The *Friday Focus* below is the second to last of the school year and one in which I seemingly contradict the *Friday Focus* in Chapter 37, which suggests that teachers are the most important people in the schoolhouse. Although we, as educators, are the most important variable in determining the extent to which our kids succeed, it is not as much about *what* we do as it is about *who* we do it for: our kids. So, it is not about us; it is about our kids. To make my point, I begin this week's *Friday Focus* by quoting the opening line of a best-selling Christian book. Clearly, this would not be advisable at all schools, but as I have stated before, each school culture is unique, and at this particular school drawing upon such a resource was not only appropriate, but affirming.

Much like the previous *Friday Focus*, my primary purpose in the one below is simply to encourage our teachers, honor them for the work they had done during the year, and remind them why we all do what we do: to make a positive difference in the lives of the kids we serve. Like most of the *Friday Focus* writings written during the latter part of the year, this one requires very little in the way of an introduction. However, I do close by again offering an excellent resource for any teacher at the school (or for any reader of this book): TED. TED stands for Technology, Entertainment, and Design and is the name of a small nonprofit organization begun in 1984. It was born out of an observation by Richard Saul Wurman, who recognized a powerful convergence between the three industries of technology, entertainment, and design. TED is devoted to what they advertise as "ideas worth sharing" and, although it has grown in scope since its inception, is still best known for its annual conference in Long Beach, California, which typically brings together the best thinkers and speakers from the worlds of technology, entertainment, and design. At the annual conference, speakers are allotted no more than twenty minutes to speak on their topic. Because I was quoting Rick Warren in this *Friday Focus,* I included a link to Warren's talk at the TED conference in 2006 (Warren, 2006).

Friday Focus!

Friday, May 16

> *It's not about you.*
> — Rick Warren (2002, p. 3)

I will go out on a limb and predict that many of you have read Rick Warren's *The Purpose-Driven Life* (2002). I chose to begin this next-to-last *Friday Focus* of the year with the very first sentence from this amazing book for a number of reasons. First, in a way, it completely contradicts the message of my last FF relating to the letter Y in which I wrote that it was all about you and that our "You variable" sets us apart from other schools. Like much in our profession, both sides of the "you" perspective are valid. On the one hand, it's not about you at all; rather, it is about our kids. At the same time, it is all about you, because a mediocre teacher and a superstar teacher could teach the exact same group of students and achieve entirely different results. One reason teachers at our school rise above all others is because they realize how important their role is, yet understand that any reward or recognition they might receive is secondary in importance to serving the kids in their classroom. It's really not about us at all, but about those children who so desperately need us to selflessly and passionately do all that we can to help them succeed as students and as human beings. In other words, our teachers are *givers*, not *takers.*

Two Fridays ago, I attended the Georgia State Teacher of the Year banquet along with Melissa Sessa. One of the speakers concluded his remarks with a nice phrase that reminded me of you: "Takers eat well, but givers sleep well." Assuming this to be true, I am most confident that teachers at our school sleep extremely well at night because we are the most giving community of educators I have ever known. We give in ways that go above and beyond, both in extraordinary ways and in ways that arise in every day teaching. For example:

- Others tell; our teachers sell.

- Others impress; our teachers influence.

- Others try to be heard; our teachers strive to be understood.

- Others explain; our teachers energize.

- Others inform; our teachers inspire.

- Others relay facts; our teachers tell stories.

In addition to the above, we give by practicing empathy. Many of our teachers succeed because they take the time to really get to know their students. It is easy to become frustrated with many of our students, our parents and—during the course of a long school year—sometimes even each other. In such instances we give again by recalling the words of Philo Judaeus from two thousand years ago: "Be kind. Everyone you meet is fighting a tough battle." Thank you for being kind, even when the recipient of this kindness may not be deserving of it at the moment.

Giving teaches us to look beyond ourselves and makes our world a better place. As an added bonus, giving makes us feel good. As teachers, we give so much of ourselves each year and—in the end—it is always worth our effort. The marks we leave in life—our legacies—are left in the lives of other people. In the case of teachers, that includes the students we teach. When those who *know* are able to *show*, those who learn are able to *grow*. Thanks for showing our kids so much about our curriculum this year. More importantly, thanks for showing them how to be good and giving people. They have grown dramatically as a result. Sleep well yet again tonight, knowing you have given much to many this year. In reflecting upon the "takers–givers" quote above, I sense that—despite the many hours I have worked while principal at our school—I may have taken more from each of you than I have given in return. If so, I leave intending to remedy that imbalance in the future by recalling all that you have given me and paying it forward to others whom I meet. The many valuable lessons you have taught me through your actions are definitely worth passing along.

Again, understanding our kids and giving them the tools they need to succeed is one way we *Taught with Passion* again this year. As a final small gift, here is a link of Warren speaking at the 2006 TED. If you can set aside 20 minutes, I think you may enjoy his message:

http://www.ted.com/index.php/talks/view/id/71

Happy Weekend!

Jeff

37

A Culture of Possibility

The Thirty-Seventh Friday

The following *Friday Focus* is, of course, the final one in this book as well as the final one I wrote as principal at Otwell Middle School. In it, I reference a Dickinson quote, which I had shared with our graduating eighth graders the evening before during an awards ceremony. It is one that aligned perfectly with our school's motto, *The Possibilities are Endless*, which, over time, became much more than just a motto and instead became a sacred part of our school's culture. Years before, we had displayed this motto all over the school. We posted college pennants from more than 200 major universities on our cafeteria wall surrounding bold letters proclaiming our motto hoping to inspire students to realize they could attend college anywhere in the world. We included our motto in many of our parent newsletters and had it printed on many staff and student school spirit shirts. Our motto was prominently displayed on our school letterhead and on a large sign in our main office. It was hard not to notice our motto if you spent any time at all visiting or reading about our school. To be honest, an occasional disgruntled parent even used the motto against us when we would not agree to something they wanted that we thought was not in the best interests of students; I recall one angry father shouting, "I guess the possibilities are *not* endless at your school" before hanging up on me!

I can just as honestly state, however, that the vast majority of teachers at our school took this motto to heart, believing in it both on an individual student basis and on a schoolwide level. On an individual basis, every single day of the school year, I witnessed many teachers staying late to work with a child who needed some form of extra support, holding their students—and themselves—accountable for learning—and teaching—important curriculum standards. I saw teachers begin to believe that a school ranked last in predicted performance (ours!) based on various demographics could actually place first in many measures of student achievement. I saw a school whose teachers agreed to voluntarily show up two Saturdays each year from 9:00 to 12:00 to work with students who had failed a test or failed to complete an assignment so that our school could be open every Saturday, staffed by at least four teachers and one administrator. I saw this school recognized time and again for its teacher and student performance. Although I have said before and will state again that the most important variable to success in a classroom is the teacher working in that classroom, to carry this from an isolated phenomenon to a schoolwide pattern of behaving requires a thriving school culture, one that shapes attitudes and beliefs and guides the actions of the educators working in the schoolhouse. As educators, whether we are classroom teachers or building administrators, we must do everything in our power to cultivate a school culture that supports the belief that, for our students, the possibilities are indeed endless.

School culture has a powerful influence on school performance. Patterson, Purkey, and Parker (1986) summarize the general knowledge base regarding school culture:

- School culture affects the behavior and achievement of elementary and secondary school students.

- School culture does not fall from the sky; it is created and thus can be manipulated by people within the school.

- School cultures are unique; whatever their commonalities, no two schools will be exactly alike—nor should they be.

- To the extent that it provides a focus and clear purpose for the school, culture becomes the cohesion that bonds the school together as it goes about its mission.

- Though we concentrate on its beneficial nature, culture can be counterproductive and an obstacle to educational success; culture can also be oppressive and discriminatory for various subgroups within the school.

- Lasting fundamental change (e.g., changes in teaching practices or the decision making structure) requires understanding and, often, altering the school's culture; cultural change is a slow process. (p. 98)

Stated directly, a school's culture can assist school improvement efforts or act as a barrier to change. It can motivate teachers to go above and beyond the call of duty or compel them to do less than they would otherwise choose to do. It can empower or inhibit risk taking. It can influence a new teacher to dedicate her life to the profession or leave after only a year. It is a contributing factor to whether a child meets standards on classroom and standardized assessments. Yes, when it comes to school culture, the possibilities are endless. I implore all educators—whatever your role—to do whatever you can in that role to work toward building a positive school culture. Dream big dreams and use your imagination to make them come true—for yourselves and for your students.

Friday Focus!

Friday, May 23

> *The possible's slow fuse is lit by the imagination.*
> — Emily Dickinson

Teachers, just a quick (due, in part, to the fact that I just realized at 7:02 A.M. that I had intended to write today's *Friday Focus*) FF, as we embark upon our final Friday of another great year of teaching and learning at our school. Last night, I shared the above Dickinson quote with our eighth graders. When I lived in Amherst, Massachusetts, many years ago, I used to enjoy the Dickinson homestead located near the town center. The quote above speaks to all of us, students and teachers alike. Another reason I like it so much is that it parallels our school motto, "The Possibilities are Endless," so nicely. Truly, we can do almost anything we set our minds to. Our students, guided by so many master teachers and extraordinary human beings, will also be able to accomplish great things. Thank you for motivating and inspiring more than 900 young people again this year.

I recently read the children's book *Dream: A Tale of Wonder, Wisdom, & Wishes* by Susan V. Bosak. Like Dickinson, she encourages young people to dream great dreams and to follow through on these dreams by believing, doing, and thinking. It is not enough to merely dream of future greatness; we must apply many hours of disciplined thought and disciplined action so that we realize our dreams. Our kids are learning this from us and will be well served, many years from now, when their own fuse becomes shorter—with resounding results! For some of the older folks on staff (e.g., moi), we are nearing the following stage of dreaming, from Bosak's book (2004):

> I have dreamed a lifetime of dreams
> I reached many of them
> Not all, but many
> Many also changed along the way.
> What I have most are fine memories
> When you're as old as I am,
> You still dream dreams
> But they're different.
> Mostly they're wishes for those who follow. (p. 29)

Like all of you, I spend a huge amount of time working at our school. I still have goals I wish to accomplish in my personal and professional life. But, honestly, my primary concern is the wishes I have for my own daughter and—to just a slightly lesser extent—every other child enrolled at our school. I know that if I hold each of them to the highest of standards and insist that they meet *my* expectations for *them*, that somewhere down the road, this will result in them meeting their own expectations, in the form of the dreams they have for their future.

Again, "possible" is a long fuse, which we must ignite and keep burning each and every day if we are to succeed. I remind you that what you do is of the utmost importance and literally *anything* you set your mind to accomplish with your students is, indeed, possible. If you do not believe this, you will need to observe Coach Jones and his class walking from his classroom to the cafeteria next year. Prior to this year, even I would have said that what happens during this time is *not* possible. He has made me a believer that *anything* we want to accomplish is possible! Thanks to each of you for another amazing year. Despite our inevitable tough times, I received more accolades about our school from parents this year than ever before. Make today the best day of the entire 180 and revel in your greatness all weekend long....

Have an Awesome Weekend!

Jeff

A Final Word

Every school has a culture, whether the principal and other building leaders are attentive to it or take any specific actions to make it as positive and productive as possible. I am a firm believer that a school's culture is every bit as impacting on its academic performance as are the programs and curriculum standards it has in place. Culture influences virtually everything that occurs within the school, from the way we celebrate our accomplishments, to the way we treat our students, to the way we communicate with our parents. Student and teacher performance will never improve unless the people working within the school feel valued and safe and are eager to share what they know with each other and learn from one another in order to achieve their collective goal of continuous self-improvement. Because of the important role school culture plays in our schools, principals—with the support of other building-level leaders—must purposefully engage all school employees in actions designed to address this critical school improvement responsibility.

The *Friday Focus* communication memo is one example of a simple, yet powerful, way to build a positive school culture. Schools use the *Friday Focus* memos tend to create cultures defined by collaboration, collegiality, consistency, and the ability to continuously improve from within, building efficacy—the belief that we *can* and *do* make a difference, both in the lives of our students and the results we achieve on state accountability tests—among all stakeholders. I encourage educators at any level who are reading this book to begin using the *Friday Focus* on a weekly basis. When you do, I predict you will find it serves as a positive and powerful tool for building your school's culture—one week at a time. Like any good work we do as professional educators, writing a weekly memo about teaching and learning requires dedicated time and concentrated effort, two commodities in short supply for most of us in education. Yet, my own experiences writing weekly *Friday Focus* memos over the past several years has proven conclusively that these extra efforts are worth it, as more and more teachers become actively involved in improving our schools. I hope you find this to be the case as well once you begin sharing your insights, expertise, and enthusiasm with your colleagues. Please contact me to let me know how the *Friday Focus* is working at your own school; lead with passion!

References

Anderson, M., & Feltenstein, T. (2009). *Change is good…you go first*. Naperville, IL: Simple Truths.

Archer, A., & Gleason, M. (1993). *Advanced skills for school success*. North Billerica, MA: Curriculum Associates.

Barth, R. (1990). *Improving schools from within: Teachers, parents, and principals can make the difference*. San Francisco, CA: Jossey-Bass.

Barth, R. (2002). The culture builder. *Educational Leadership, 59*(8), 6–11.

Biemans, H. J., Deel, O. R., & Simons, P. R. (2001). Differences between successful and less successful students while working with the CONTACT-2 strategy. *Learning and Instruction 11*, 265–282.

Blackburn, B. (2007). *Classroom instruction from A to Z: How to promote student learning*. Larchmont, New York, NY: Eye On Education.

Blanchard, K., & Stoner, J. (2004). *Full steam ahead!: Unleash the power of vision in your work and your life*. San Francisco, CA: Berrett-Koehler.

Bluestein, J. (2008). *Making homework work: Building flexibility into your homework policy*. Retrieved August 20, 2008, from http://www.janebluestein.com/articles/hw_flex.html

Bosak, S. V. (2004). *Dream: A tale of wonder, wisdom & wishes*. Stoufville, ON: TCP.

Brandt, R. (1998), *Powerful learning*. Alexandria, VA: Association for Supervision and Curriculum Development.

Bruner, J. S. (1961). The act of discovery. *Harvard Educational Review 31*(1), 21–32.

Cameron, J., & Pierce, W.D. (1994). Reinforcement, reward, and intrinsic motivation: A meta-analysis. *Review of Educational Research, 64*, 363–423.

Chestnut Oaks Middle School. (2008). *Graphic organizers*. Retrieved June 12, 2008, from http://coms.sumter17.k12.sc.us/site_res_view_folder.aspx?id=d2274d4d-2e4e-4839-8edf-8b10cb4fca28

Chickering, A. W., & Gamson, Z. F. (1987). Seven principles for good practice in undergraduate education. *American Association of Higher Education Bulletin, 39*, 3–7.

Collins, J. (2001). *Good to great: Why some companies make the leap…and others don't*. New York, NY: Harper Collins.

Collins, J. (2005). *Good to great and the social sectors: A monograph to accompany Good to great*. New York, NY: Harper Collins.

Cooper, H. A. (2006). *The battle over homework: Common ground for administrators, teachers, and parents*. Thousand Oaks, CA: Corwin.

Covey, S. R. (1989). *The 7 habits of highly effective people: Powerful lessons in personal change*. New York, NY: Simon and Schuster.

Covey, S. R., Merrill, A. R., & Merrill, R. R. (1996). *First things first: To live, to love, to learn, to leave a legacy*. New York, NY: Free Press.

Crane, T. G. (2007). *The heart of coaching: Using transformational coaching to create a high-performance coaching culture*. San Diego: F. T. A.

Craske, M. L. (1985). Improving persistence through observational learning and attribution retraining. *British Journal of Educational Psychology, 55*, 138–147.

Cunningham, P. (1999). *Phonics they use: Words for reading and writing*. New York, NY: Longman.

Curriculum Associates (2009). *Advanced skills for school success*. Retrieved June 2, 2009, from www.curriculumassociates.com

Darling-Hammond, L., & Ifill-Lynch, O. (2006). If they'd only do their work. *Educational Leadership, 65*(3), 8–13.

Denton, D. R. (2000). *Teaching all children to read*. Atlanta, GA: Southern Regional Education Board. (ED 440364)

Devaney, L. (2009). *RTI: Not just for special education*. Retrieved June 2, 2009, from http://www.eschoolnews.com/news/top-news/news-by-subject/school- administration/?i=58281

Dochy, F. Segers, M., & Buehl, M. M. (1999). The relation between assessment practices And outcomes of studies: The case of research on prior knowledge. *Review of Educational Research, 69*(2), 145–186.

Douglas, M. (1985). Introduction. In J. L. Gross & S. Rayner, *Measuring culture: A paradigm for the analysis of social organization*. New York, NY: Columbia University.

DuFour, R., DuFour, R., Eaker, R., & Karhanek, G. (2004). *Whatever it takes: How professional learning communities respond when kids don't learn*. Bloomington, IN: Solution Tree.

DuFour, R., DuFour, R., Eaker, R., & Many, T. (2006). *Learning by doing: A Handbook for professional learning communities at work*. Bloomington, IN: Solution Tree.

DuFour, R., & Eaker, R. (1998). *Professional learning communities at work: Best practices for enhancing student achievement*. Bloomington, IN: Solution Tree.

Eaker, R., DuFour, R., & DuFour, R. (2002). *Getting started: Reculturing schools to become professional learning communities*. Bloomington, IN: Solution Tree.

Eaker, R. (2009, August). *Developing a stretch culture*. Presentation at Professional Learning Communities at Work Institute, Lincolnshire, IL.

Earl, L. M. (2003). *Assessment as learning: Using classroom assessment to maximize student learning*. Thousand Oaks, CA: Corwin.

Eastwood, K.W., & Louis, K.S. (1992). Restructuring that lasts: Managing the performance dip. *Journal of School Leadership, 2*(2), 212–224.

Edmonds, R. (1986). Characteristics of effective schools. In U. Neisser (Ed.), *The school achievement of minority children: New perspectives* (pp. 93–104). Hillsdale, NJ: Lawrence Erlbaum.

Esquith, R. (2003). *There are no shortcuts*. New York, NY: Pantheon.

Esquith, R. (2007). *Teach like your hair's on fire: The methods and madness inside room 56.* New York, NY: Penguin.

Faber, S. (2006). *How to teach reading when you're not a reading teacher.* Nashville, TN: Incentive Publications.

Friedman, T. L. (2006). *The world is flat: A brief history of the twenty-first century.* New York, NY: Farrar, Straus, and Giroux.

Fullan, M. (2001). *Leading in a culture of change.* San Francisco, CA: Jossey-Bass.

Fullan, M. (2008). *The six secrets of change: What the best leaders do to help their organizations survive and thrive.* San Francisco, CA: Jossey-Bass.

Georgia Department of Education (2008). *School keys: Unlocking excellence through the Georgia school standards.* Retrieved June 21, 2008, from http://public.doek12.ga.us/DMGetDocument.aspx/SCHOOL%20KEYS%20FINAL%205–29–07.pdf?p=6CC6799F8C1371F6175E5B6E474BB7C617F852E1ADE57E7942B6D677375DA861&Type=D

Glickman, C. D. (1998). *Supervision of instruction: A developmental approach.* Boston, MA: Allyn & Bacon.

Hall, T., & Strangman, N. (2002). *Graphic organizers.* Wakefield, MA: National Center on Accessing Curriculum. Retrieved June 28, 2008, from http:www.cast.org/publications/ncac/ncac_go.html

Hanson, M. (2001). Institutional theory and educational change. *Education Administration Quarterly, 37*(5), 637–661.

Heath, C., & Heath, D. (2007a). *Made to stick: Why some ideas survive and others die.* New York, NY: Random House.

Heath, C., & Heath, D. (2007b). *Teaching that sticks.* Retrieved August 21, 2008, from http://www.madetostick.com/teachers/

Howard, J. (1990). *Getting smart: The social construction of intelligence.* Lexington, MA: The Efficacy Institute.

Ikeda, M. J., Rahn-Blakeslee, A., Niebling, B. C., Allison, R., & Stumme, J. (2006). Evaluating evidence-based practice in response-to-intervention systems. *NASP Communiqué, 34*(8), 28–38.

Internet4classrooms (2008). *Differentiated instruction.* Retrieved July 12, 2009, from http://www.internet4classrooms.com/di.htm

Jackson, R. R. (2009). *Never work harder than your students and other principles of great teaching.* Alexandria, VA: Association for Supervision and Curriculum Development.

Johnson, G. (1992). Managing strategic change: Strategy, culture, and action. *Long Range Planning, 25*(1), 28–36.

Kohn, A. (2006). *The homework myth: Why our kids get too much of a bad thing.* Cambridge, MA: De Capo.

Kouzes, J. M., & Posner, B. Z. (2003). *Encouraging the heart: A leader's guide to rewarding and recognizing others.* San Francisco, CA: Jossey-Bass.

Kouzes, J. M., & Posner, B. Z. (2008). *The leadership challenge.* San Francisco, CA: Jossey-Bass.

Lencioni, P. (2002). *The five dysfunctions of a team: A leadership fable.* San Francisco, CA: Jossey-Bass.

Little, J. W. (1982). Norms of collegiality and experimentation: Workplace conditions of school success. *American Educational Research Journal, 19,* 325–340.

Marzano, R. J. (2007). *The art and science of teaching: A comprehensive framework for effective instruction.* Alexandria, VA: Association for Supervision and Curriculum Development.

Marzano, R. J. (2003). *What works in schools: Translating research into action.* Alexandria, VA: Association for Supervision and Curriculum Development.

Marzano, R. J. (2004). *Building background knowledge for academic achievement.* Alexandria, VA: Association for Supervision and Curriculum Development.

Marzano, R. J., & Pickering, D. (2005). *Building academic vocabulary: Teachers' manual.* Alexandria, VA: Association for Supervision and Curriculum Development.

Marzano, R. J., Pickering, D., & Pollock, J. E. (2001) *Classroom instruction that works: Research-based strategies for increasing student achievement.* Alexandria, VA: Association for Supervision and Curriculum Development.

Marzano, R. J., Waters, T., & McNulty, B. A. (2005). *School leadership that works: From research to results.* Alexandria, VA: Association for Supervision and Curriculum Development.

Maxwell, J. C. (2002). *Leadership 101: What every leader needs to know.* Nashville, TN: Thomas Nelson.

Meyers, C., & Jones, T. B. (1993). *Case studies promoting active learning: Strategies for the college classroom.* San Francisco, CA: Jossey-Bass.

Moore, D. W., & Readance, J. E. (1984). A quantitative and qualitative review of graphic organizer research. *Journal of Educational Research, 78*(1), 11–17.

Nanus, B. (1992). *Visionary leadership.* San Francisco, CA: Jossey-Bass.

National Association of Directors of Special Education (NASDSE). (2005). *Response to intervention: Policy considerations and implementation.* Alexandria, VA: Author.

National Commission on Excellence in Education. (1983). *A nation at risk: The imperative for educational reform.* Washington, DC: U.S. Government Printing Office. (ED 226 006)

Oliva, P. F. (1997). *Developing the curriculum.* New York, NY: Addison-Wesley Longman.

Patterson, J. L., Purkey, S. C., & Parker, J. V. (1986). *Productive school systems for a nonrational world.* Alexandria, VA: Association for Supervision and Curriculum Development.

Perkins, D. (1995). *Outsmarting IQ: The emerging science of learnable intelligence.* New York, NY: Free Press.

Pfeffer, J., & Sutton, R. I. (2000). *The knowing-doing gap: How smart companies turn knowledge into action.* Boston, MA: Harvard Business.

Phillips, L. V. (1987). Closure: The fine art of making learning stick. *Instructor, 97*(3), 36–38.

Pollock, J. E. (2007). *Improving student learning one teacher at a time.* Alexandria, VA: Association for Supervision and Curriculum Development.

Public Agenda. (2000). *Survey finds little sign of backlash against academic standards or standardized tests.* New York, NY: Author.

Resnick, L. B. (2001, Fall). The mismeasure of learning. *Education Next.* Retrieved June 29, 2009, from http://www.umd.umich.edu/casl/natsci/faculty/zitzewitz/curie/TeacherPrep/72.pdf

Rosentahl, R., & Jacobson, L. (1968). *Pygmalion in the classroom.* New York, NY: Holt, Rinehart, and Winston.

Saphier, J. (2005). Effort-based ability. In R. DuFour, R. Eaker, & R. DuFour (Eds.), *On common ground* (pp. 85–113). Bloomington, IN: Solution Tree.

Saphier, J., & Gower, R. (1997). *The skillful teacher.* Acton, MA: Research for Better Teaching.

Saphier, J., & King, M. (1985). Good seeds grow in strong cultures. *Educational Leadership, 42* (6), 67–74.

Schlechty, P. (2002). *Working on the work: An action plan for teachers, principals, and superintendents.* San Francisco, CA: Jossey-Bass.

Schmoker, M. (1999). *Results: The key to continuous school improvement.* Alexandria, VA: Association for Supervision and Curriculum Development.

Schmoker, M. (2006). *Results now: How we can achieve unprecedented improvements in teaching and learning.* Alexandria, VA: Association for Supervision and Curriculum Development.

Seligman, M. (1990). *Learned optimism: How to change your mind and your life.* New York, NY: Pocket Books.

Seligman, M. (1994). *What you can change and what you can't.* New York, NY: Knopf.

Senge, P., Cambron-McCabe, N., Lucas, T., Smith, B., Dutton, J., & Kleiner, A. (2000). *Schools that learn: A fifth discipline fieldbook for educators, parents, and everyone who cares about education.* New York, NY: Doubleday.

Slattery, P. (1995). *Curriculum development in the postmodern era.* New York, NY: Garland.

Smith, R. (2004). *Conscious classroom management: Unlocking the secrets of great teaching.* Fairfax, CA: Conscious Teaching.

St. John, R. (2005). *Stupid, ugly, unlucky, and rich: Spike's guide to success.* Toronto: Train of Thought Arts.

Tapscott, D., & Williams, A. D. (2008). *Wikinomics: How mass collaboration changes everything.* New York, NY: Penguin.

Tomlinson, C. A. (1995). *How to differentiate instruction in mixed-ability classrooms.* Alexandria, VA: Association for Supervision and Curriculum Development.

Tomlinson, C. A. (1999). *The differentiated classroom: Responding to the needs of all learners*. Alexandria, VA: Association for Supervision and Curriculum Development.

Tomlinson, C. A., & McTighe, J. (2006). *Integrating differentiated instruction and Understanding by design*. Alexandria, VA: Association for Supervision and Curriculum Development.

Urdan, T., Midgley, C., & Anderman, E. (1998). The role of classroom goal structure In students' use of self-handicapping strategies. *American Educational Research Journal, 35*, 101–122.

U.S. Department of Education. (1986). *What works*. Washington, DC: Author.

Van Overwalle, F., & De Metsenaere, M. 1990. The effects of attribution-based intervention and study strategy training on academic achievement in college freshmen. *British Journal of Educational Psychology, 60*, 299–311.

Warren, R. (2002). *The purpose-driven life: What on Earth am I here for?* Grand Rapids, MI: Zondervan.

Warren, R. (2006). *A life of purpose*. Retrieved July 21, 2008, from http://www.ted.com/talks/rick_warren_on_a_life_of_purpose.html

West-Burnham, J. (1992). *Managing quality in schools*, London, UK: Longman.

Whitaker, T. (2002). *What great principals do differently: Fifteen things that matter most*. Larchmont, NY: Eye On Education.

Whitaker, T. (2004). *What great teachers do differently: Fourteen things that matter most*. Larchmont, NY: Eye On Education.

Whitaker, T., & Lumpa, D. (2004). *Great quotes for great educators*. Larchmont, NY: Eye On Education.

Whitaker, T, Whitaker, B., & Lumpa, D. (2000). *Motivating and inspiring teachers: The educational leader's guide for building staff morale*. Larchmont, NY: Eye On Education.

Whitaker, T., & Zoul, J. (2008). *The 4 core factors for school success*. Larchmont, NY: Eye On Education.

White, M. A. (1999). *Visual literacy*. Retrieved June, 2, 2008, from http://www.bham.wednet.edu/vislit.html

Wilmette District 39. (2008). What others are saying about D.I. Retrieved June 1, 2008, from http://www.wilmette39.org/DI39/quotes.html

Wolf, P., & Supon, V. (1994). *Winning through student participation in lesson closure*. Retrieved July 15, 2008, from http://www.eric.ed.gov/ERICDocs/data/ericdocs2sql/content_storage_01/0000019b/80/15/73/33.pdf

Wong H., & Wong, R. (1998). *The first days of school: How to be an effective teacher*. Mountain View, CA: Harry K. Wong.

Zoul, J. (2006). *Improving your school one week at a time: Building the foundation for professional teaching and learning*. Larchmont, NY: Eye On Education.